Included in the series:*

* Also published in French. Other titles to appear.

National strategies for e-learning in post-secondary education and training

Tony Bates

Paris 2001
UNESCO: International Institute for Educational Planning

The Swedish International Development Co-operation Agency (Sida) has provided financial assistance for the publication of this booklet.

Published in 2001 by the United Nations
Educational, Scientific and Cultural Organization
7 place de Fontenoy, F 75352 Paris 07 SP
Printed in France by Imprimerie Alençonnaise
Cover design by Pierre Finot

ISBN 92-803-1214-6

Fundamentals of educational planning

The booklets in this series are written primarily for two types of clientele: those engaged in educational planning and administration, in developing as well as developed countries; and others, less specialized, such as senior government officials and policy-makers who seek a more general understanding of educational planning and of how it is related to overall national development. They are intended to be of use either for private study or in formal training programmes.

Since this series was launched in 1967 practices and concepts of educational planning have undergone substantial change. Many of the assumptions which underlay earlier attempts to rationalize the process of educational development have been criticized or abandoned. Even if rigid mandatory centralized planning has now clearly proven to be inappropriate, this does not mean that all forms of planning have been dispensed with. On the contrary, the need for collecting data, evaluating the efficiency of existing programmes, undertaking a wide range of studies, exploring the future and fostering broad debate on these bases to guide educational policy and decision-making has become even more acute than before. One cannot make sensible policy choices without assessing the present situation, specifying the goals to be reached, marshalling the means to attain them and monitoring what has been accomplished. Hence planning is also a way to organize learning: by mapping, targeting, acting and correcting.

The scope of educational planning has been broadened. In addition to the formal system of education, it is now applied to all other important educational efforts in non-formal settings. Attention to the growth and expansion of education systems is being complemented and sometimes even replaced by a growing concern for the quality of the entire educational process and for the control of its results. Finally, planners and administrators have become more and more aware of the importance of implementation strategies and of the role of different regulatory mechanisms in this respect: the choice of financing methods, the examination and certification procedures or various other regulation and incentive structures. The concern of planners is twofold: to reach a better understanding of the validity of education in its own empirically observed specific dimensions and to help in defining appropriate strategies for change.

The purpose of these booklets includes monitoring the evolution and change in educational policies and their effect upon educational planning requirements; highlighting current issues of educational planning and analyzing them in the context of their historical and societal setting; and disseminating methodologies of planning which can be applied in the context of both the developed and the developing countries.

For policy-making and planning, vicarious experience is a potent source of learning: the problems others face, the objectives they seek, the routes they try, the results they arrive at and the unintended results they produce are worth analysis.

In order to help the Institute identify the real up-to-date issues in educational planning and policy-making in different parts of the world, an Editorial Board has been appointed, composed of two general editors and associate editors from different regions, all professionals of high repute in their own field. At the first meeting of this new Editorial Board in January 1990, its members identified key topics to be covered in the coming issues under the following headings:

1. Education and development.
2. Equity considerations.
3. Quality of education.
4. Structure, administration and management of education.
5. Curriculum.
6. Cost and financing of education.
7. Planning techniques and approaches.
8. Information systems, monitoring and evaluation.

Each heading is covered by one or two associate editors.

The series has been carefully planned but no attempt has been made to avoid differences or even contradictions in the views expressed by the authors. The Institute itself does not wish to impose any official doctrine. Thus, while the views are the responsibility of the authors and may not always be shared by UNESCO or the IIEP, they warrant attention in the international forum of ideas. Indeed, one of the purposes of this series is to reflect a diversity of experience and opinions by giving different authors from a wide range of backgrounds and disciplines the opportunity of expressing their views on changing theories and practices in educational planning.

Today, more and more countries are moving towards a knowledge-based economy. In such economies, the workforce must be capable of learning continuously, be familiar with techniques of accessing and processing information, and possess excellent communication skills.

E-learning, or the use of new information and communication technologies in education, is both the fruit of these changes, and the means of assimilating them. Far more than a mere tool to enhance educational delivery, it provides the increased flexibility, easy communication, and immediate access to global resources that learners, as well as their trainers, need and indeed demand.

However, planners and policy-makers may rightly ask whether e-learning is a vital issue in many developing countries, where the economy may still be based on agriculture and low-tech industries, and resources are limited. Yet they cannot afford to ignore that foreign e-learning programmes may represent a threat to national educational institutions, culture and language.

The author sets out the key questions that must be tackled when designing e-learning policy strategies. To what extent should e-learning be regulated/deregulated? How to strike a balance between public and private providers? What are the issues at stake in financing e-learning?

It is clear that there is no set model for regulating the development of e-learning, and strategies will depend on the situation of each country. However, policy-makers and administrators alike will find this booklet a very useful guide in defining the most appropriate way forward. The IIEP is grateful to Tony Bates for this insightful and valuable contribution to the debate on e-learning.

Gudmund Hernes
Director, IIEP

Preface

New information and communication technologies have revolutionized the world economy, contributing significantly to the globalization of trade, capital and corporate management.

Will education be affected in the same way as markets, banking services and information? It is now very easy in most developed countries, and even in a number of developing countries, to log onto the Web site of a university in order to enrol as an e-learner and obtain a degree, without having to travel great distances in order to do so. What will be the consequences of these technological advances? Although many will be positive, others will perhaps be less so.

Amongst the foreseeable advantages of e-learning is that it will enhance the ability of educators to address different audiences and allow them to diversify their teaching style. Many courses are given by international professors or experts, who have had to develop excellent training materials in order to overcome the obstacles of distance and absence of contact with students, and who use innovative teaching methods in order to maintain students' interest. The competition that is thus generated with the traditional teaching methods used in many national or local institutions can only be of benefit to all students. Another advantage is that of promoting lifelong learning. It is no longer necessary to stop working, nor to leave the workplace, in order to be able to pursue further studies. Thus many students will be able to follow university courses from home, and employees will be able to take a training course whilst at work as long as their employer is willing to grant them the time to do so. E-learning is a chance for lifelong education to become a reality, and not a mere slogan.

E-learning is nevertheless the source of much debate. Education cannot be looked upon as a mere product to be bought and sold in the same way as one would buy a book, a compact disc or a car. Education transmits values, contributes to forging national identity, and to strengthening national integration and solidarity. Thus the question arises of whether the content of a country's school and university programmes, and the values to be transmitted, should be left in the hands of private enterprise or foreign universities. Many governments, aware of this fact and conscious of the issues at stake, may well feel the need to create a national e-learning system. This booklet provides very useful information in this regard. However Tony Bates warns the reader: developing e-learning is costly – it requires know-how, access to state-of-the-art technologies, design of content, preparation of appropriate teaching materials, and the maintenance of a set of educators and trainers, who can tutor students on-line and/or at a centre designated for that purpose. Both for the sake of sharing costs and providing an adequate supply of courses, building partnerships with other institutions is crucial.

Of course e-learning is more than just on-line distance education. Any programme that uses information and communication technology to enhance the learning process may be considered to fall into the category of e-learning. It is in particular the use of the Internet and the Web in the teaching and learning process, at all levels, that constitutes a major breakthrough whose advantages have yet to be fully explored.

The present booklet focuses on post-secondary education and training, the field in which most new development has occurred in recent years. E-learning is not a passing phenomenon. It will continue to develop, and will bring about fundamental changes in the provision of education at post-secondary level, both for school-leavers and lifelong learners. All planners and policy-makers will sooner or later be confronted with the need to make informed decisions about e-learning. This booklet, written in a simple and accessible style, will help them to do so.

Françoise Caillods
Co-General Editor

Acknowledgements

This report makes heavy use of the work of others and previously published work of my own. I am particularly indebted to Glen Farrell and the Commonwealth of Learning for permission to use parts of a paper I did earlier this year for them for their publication, 'The Changing Face of Virtual Education'. I am also grateful to Jim Mingle, formerly Executive Director of the State Higher Education Executive Officers Association, for permission to include some of his work and ideas that he developed in project reports for the States of Maine and Indiana in the USA. I would also like to thank James Fulcher, from Human Resources Development Canada, for his critical comments on an earlier draft. As always, though, final responsibility for the content, errors and omissions belong with the author.

Contents

List of figures

I. The growth of e-learning technologies: revolution or evolution?

There is a long history, not always glorious, of using technology to support teaching and learning in post-secondary education. In most cases, technology has been used to supplement classroom teaching. The slate, blackboard and chalk, textbooks, flip-charts, laboratory equipment, radio, film, television, the overhead projector, and computers have all been used in this way. Computers are now commonly used for PowerPoint presentations to deliver lectures, and the Internet is now being used more and more to access Web sites to support lectures.

Technology used in this way does not replace either the teacher or the classroom. Using technology to supplement classroom teaching does not radically change teaching methods. It merely enhances what would be done in the classroom in any case.

In most cases, such use of technology has increased the costs of teaching. As well as the cost of the equipment, teachers need more preparation time. In return, students may be grateful for an improvement in the presentational qualities of teachers' notes, and classes may be more interesting as a result of the use of sound and pictures, but it would be hard to show a quantifiable correlation between this use of technology and improved learning outcomes (see for instance, Russell, 1999).

However, the advent of technologies such as the Internet, computer-based multimedia, and the World Wide Web, has resulted in some significant changes in teaching and learning in post-secondary education and training. The Internet, computer-based multimedia, and the World Wide Web are the underlying technologies of 'e-learning', an emerging term used to describe the applications of such 'electronic' technologies to learning. (For a more detailed analysis of the technologies of e-learning, see Chapter 2.)

Some have argued that 'e-learning' is of a revolutionary nature, resulting in a paradigm shift, no less, comparable to the invention of the printing press in its significance for education (for example, Harasim et al., 1995). What is not in question is that those concerned with national planning for post-secondary education and training need to give at least as much consideration to the potential and implications of e-learning as to campus buildings and facilities.

This monograph looks at the potential of e-learning for post-secondary education and training, and focuses on the planning and management implications of e-learning. While the focus is on developing countries, many of the issues are universal.

The monograph is aimed primarily at those responsible for national and institutional planning at a post-secondary level. This is likely to include:

• ministers and senior civil servants in Ministries of (Advanced) Education;
• university and college Presidents/Vice-Chancellors, and university and college Vice-Presidents/senior managers responsible for academic affairs, student services, and information technology.

The monograph is likely also to be of interest to deans of faculties, specialists in the area of learning technologies, such as directors of learning technology and distance education units, librarians, and directors of related information technology departments in universities and post-secondary colleges.

This booklet looks at some of the strategies being developed to facilitate or regulate the development of e-learning. While the benefits and dangers of each strategy are discussed in this booklet, readers will have to decide for themselves how appropriate these strategies are for their own countries. In particular, the reader will have to examine very carefully the ideological and cultural implications of the application of e-learning to post-secondary education and training, and whether this conflicts with the reader's own ideological or cultural position.

E-learning is still relatively new, even in the USA. The first Web-based post-secondary education course appeared only in 1995. There are few or no locally developed e-learning initiatives in many countries, and therefore it has been difficult to find many examples of successful practice outside the most economically developed countries. Even in some of these countries, e-learning hardly exists in any systematic form.

In other words, e-learning is very much a product of a particular, mainly American, culture and economy, at a particular time. Inevitably, then, most of the examples will come from the three countries where the application of e-learning has been the most extensive: the USA, Canada and Australia. This does not necessarily mean that e-learning has no potential for other ideologies, cultures, or economies, but the strategies set out in this booklet need to be carefully analyzed for contextual relevance, and almost certainly need to be adapted to local situations. The issue of the appropriateness and the timing of e-learning for a particular nation, economy or culture is discussed in more detail in the last chapter.

How e-learning is being used

Many institutions worldwide, but particularly in North America, Australia and New Zealand, and in several European countries, such as the United Kingdom, Norway, Denmark and the Netherlands, have started to invest heavily in e-learning. E-learning is being used in three main ways in universities and colleges.

➀ *Technology-enhanced classroom teaching*

First, the Web and the Internet have been integrated into classroom teaching in the same way as previous technologies. Teachers may build a course Web page, with links through the Internet to relevant resources on other Web sites. Instructors can convert their PowerPoint slide presentations to pdf files (electronic documents), which students can download and print from a Web site. A professor may go further and construct a course Web site that includes the professor's own papers, or research materials such as photographs or slides, as well as links to other relevant sources. Teachers may also use other Web sites for illustration within their classroom lectures. And students may be asked to participate in on-line discussion forums, to discuss the lecture afterwards amongst themselves. Enhancing classroom teaching is still by far the most prevalent use of the Web in post-secondary education.

⤷ *Distance education*

Major and highly reputable universities with large on-campus teaching programmes, such as Queens University in Canada, the University of London in the United Kingdom, and the University of Wisconsin in the USA, have been offering distance education programmes for over 100 years. Institutions such as these that offer both campus-based and distance education programmes are called 'dual-mode'.

The main institutions in the USA historically involved in distance education have been the old land-grant universities, such as Penn State University and the University of Wisconsin. These and other institutions with an original mandate to serve all the citizens of their state or province, such as the University of British Columbia and the University of Saskatchewan in Canada, have tended to develop a distance education operation to complement their on-campus teaching. For such institutions, extension beyond the campus has been critical to their mandate, and hence distance education is one of several means used to reach out to farmers, working professionals, and those who cannot afford to move to a campus away from their homes or jobs. (See Mugridge and Kaufman, 1986, and Rumble and Harry, 1982, for more details on the history of dual-mode institutions.)

It has been relatively easy for these dual-mode institutions in countries with a good telecommunications infrastructure to move to on-line distance delivery. In particular, on-line discussion forums provide a quality of interaction between students at a distance that is not possible for the old print-based correspondence-type courses. Nevertheless there are many dual-mode distance education operations that are still mainly print-based, although even these are increasingly adding some on-line components, such as e-mail, to support the print materials.

In contrast to the dual-mode institutions, Daniel (1998) has described the large, dedicated distance education institutions ('single-mode') such as the British Open University, the UNED in Spain, the Chinese Central Radio and Television University, Universitas Terbuka in Indonesia, and the Korean National Open University. These are characterized by very large enrolments (usually more than 100,000 students), and the use of mass communications technology, such as print and broadcasting.

Their main mandate is to widen access, reaching out to students who cannot gain access to conventional universities (hence the term 'open'). These large distance education institutions tend to operate on a national or, increasingly, in the case of the British Open University, on an international basis. Because of the very large student enrolments, high fixed costs and low marginal costs, they bring major economies of scale to their operation, resulting in an average cost per student well below those of conventional campus-based institutions or even dual-mode distance education operations.

However, single-mode institutions have a huge investment in mass communications technologies, such as print production and broadcasting, and their primary mandate is to widen access. Thus it has been less easy for them to put a lot of their courses on-line, because the majority of the students they are targeting do not have access to the Internet at home or work. The main exceptions amongst the single-mode distance institutions are Athabasca University in Canada and the Open University of Catalonia in Spain. Athabasca University has been able to move extensively into on-line distance education, because of the wide availability of the Internet in Canadian homes. The Open University of Catalonia was created in 1994 from the beginning as an on-line virtual university. However, both of these institutions are also substantially smaller in operation than most single-mode distance institutions.

③ Distributed learning

With both technology-enhanced classroom teaching and distance education, the move to on-line learning could be seen as evolutionary, a natural next step forward in two long but separate historical processes. The potentially revolutionary development is in distributed learning, because this will radically change the way that traditional campus institutions operate.

Distributed learning describes a mix of deliberately reduced face-to-face teaching and on-line learning (for instance one face-to-face lecture or seminar a week, with the rest of the teaching and learning done on-line, replacing the traditional three face-to-face lectures a week). Unfortunately, especially in the USA, the term 'distributed learning' is also commonly used to include fully distance courses taught totally on-line. It might be more helpful to describe the mix of reduced face-to-face teaching and on-line teaching as 'mixed mode'. Another term, used in Australia, is flexible learning. While 'flexible learning' may encompass on-line learning, it can also include face-to-face teaching delivered in the workplace, and other flexible delivery methods.

Figure 1.   Continuum of on-line learning applications

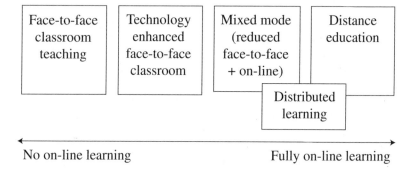

These semantic differences are confusing. The most helpful way to regard the differences is as a continuum, with 'pure' face-to-face teaching at one end, and 'pure' distance teaching at the other, with an increasing mix of on-line learning from one end of the continuum to the other (see *Figure 1*).

The significance of the mixed mode operation is that it enables the benefits of both the campus and on-line learning to be combined. It is perhaps not surprising then that the University of Central Florida in the USA reports that grades are higher when face-to-face classes are combined with on-line learning (mixed mode), compared with straight face-to-face teaching or solely distance education courses (Dziuban et al., 1999).

In this report we use the term e-learning to cover all these forms of on-line learning, including its use in private-sector training.

Reasons for the growth in e-learning

In universities and colleges throughout North America, Western Europe, and Australia, many professors are now using the Internet and the Web as an integral part of their teaching. For instance WebCT Inc., one of the main vendors of software for creating courses on the Web, claims to have licensed within four years 2,200 institutions in 81 countries to use WebCT, totalling more than 10 million student licences (www.WebCT.com/company, 31 July 2001). The merchant banker Merrill Lynch has described e-learning (the combination of the corporate learning and higher education markets) as a US$18 billion market by 2003, compared with a $2.3 billion market in 2000 (Moe and Blodget, 2000).

There are several reasons for this phenomenal growth in the use of the Web in post-secondary education and training. They can be classified roughly as instructional and social/economic.

The following are the main instructional reasons for the use of the Internet and the Web:

- access to educational resources from outside the institution on a global and instant basis;
- increased and flexible interaction with students through e-mail and discussion forums;
- course notes, diagrams, reading lists and other course materials available to students at any time;
- ability to combine text, graphics and a limited amount of multimedia, enabling a wide range of educational applications;
- professional/subject discipline links on an international basis for research and teaching purposes;

- opportunities for international, cross-cultural and collaborative learning;
- ease of creating materials and courses through low cost, off-the-shelf software such as WebCT and Blackboard;
- organization of course materials through on-line 'portals' (one-stop shopping for students for all learning resources);
- relatively low cost for teachers in terms of technology.

The social and economic reasons are more complex. Perhaps the most important is that in a knowledge-based economy students need to learn how to use technology to seek, organize, analyze and apply information appropriately. Knowledge-based economies, for instance those dependent on hi-tech sectors such as computing, telecommunications and biotechnology, and service industries, such as financial services, health, entertainment, hospitality and tourism, require a highly flexible and adaptable workforce that can continually change as the world changes around them. Thus the new knowledge-based industries require not only technology-skilled workers with up-to-date and recent knowledge, but also workers who are constantly learning, in order for such companies to compete effectively.

These changes in the workforce and the demand for more flexibility from students and employers directly influence the kind of learning and hence the kind of teaching now increasingly in demand from both students and employers in knowledge-based economies. The Conference Board of Canada has summarized well these skills (1991):

- good communication skills (reading/writing/speaking/listening);
- ability to learn independently;
- social skills: ethics, positive attitudes, responsibility;
- teamwork;
- ability to adapt to changing circumstances;
- thinking skills: problem-solving, critical/logical/numerical thinking;
- knowledge navigation: where to get/how to process information.

It might be argued that these are not very different from the kind of skills one would expect from any traditional liberal arts programme. The catch however is that these skills are required *in addition to* specialist qualifications in engineering, management, health sciences, etc.

In knowledge-based economies, 'lifelong learning' has become critical for economic development. Education and training therefore does not stop with a B.A., an M.Sc., or even a Ph.D. Learning needs to be literally for life.

A typical lifelong learner is someone working mainly full-time, in a high-tech or service industry, with a family and a rich social and personal life. Such a learner requires 'just-in-time' and personally relevant content delivered conveniently and flexibly. Such potential students or their employers are able and willing to pay the price necessary to obtain the knowledge and qualifications they need. If they are professionals, they need access to the latest research and developments in their field.

Any single cohort of students leaving university after going to university straight from school in any one year constitute approximately 2.5 per cent of the workforce in the more economically advanced countries. The remaining 97.5 per cent already in the workforce are potentially lifelong learners. Many of them will already have graduated from university or college. Lifelong learners will be more interested in small modules and short programmes, in qualifications that can be built from short modules or courses, and in learning that can be done at home and fitted around work, family and social obligations.

They will want their experience and knowledge taken into account with regard not just to admission to programmes, but to their participation and contribution to knowledge creation. Their experience in work and 'real' life is as important to them as the professor's research knowledge. They will want to be measured by what they can do, as well as what they know.

Much of lifelong learning will be incidental, picked up on the job, learning from workplace colleagues, or finding new solutions to particular problems as encountered. For most of these lifelong learners, it is not desirable or practical to go back to university or college campuses full time for re-training or up-dating. Nevertheless, at a

✓ conservative estimate, **the lifelong learning market for formal university and college courses in knowledge-based economies is at least as great as the market for students leaving high school for university and college** (see Bates, 2000, pp. 7-13, for more discussion of this issue).

✓ **E-learning is an ideal mode of delivery for lifelong learners.** It provides the access and flexibility that they need. It also allows for experienced students to share and apply their knowledge through the use of discussion forums.

Lifelong learners are also a market that has become extremely attractive to the private sector. Because most lifelong learners are working full time, they have greater disposable income than high school leavers. The private sector therefore tends to see e-learning as just another sub-set of e-commerce. It is the private training sector in particular that is responsible for a major part of the growth in e-learning. However, there are areas of the lifelong learning market that need input from the public sector as well. Continuing professional education for instance needs access to the latest research and developments in professional fields and the knowledge required will rest largely with universities and colleges.

In knowledge-based economies – or in those aspiring to be knowledge-based – how best to encourage lifelong learning and how best to determine and regulate the role of the private and public sectors in e-learning are major challenges for government. This issue will be returned to later.

So what's new?

Is the advent of the Internet and the World Wide Web really leading to a paradigm shift in teaching in higher education? Have we not heard this story before? Were not radio, then film, then television, then computers, all going to revolutionize higher education, and what happened? A lot of usually foreign equipment was bought, staff trained, then after the novelty wore off, it was forgotten. Especially for developing countries, the main result was increased debt and little material benefit. In particular, while there were many successful pilot projects, the extensive use of technology as a replacement for traditional teaching has not in general been successful or sustainable (see for instance Arnove, 1976).

There is certainly a good deal of hyperbole and hysteria in the USA in particular about the benefits and dangers of the Internet and the Web for teaching in higher education. It will be seen that for many developing countries, there are major barriers that will prevent the extensive use of on-line learning. Nevertheless, **there is a fundamental shift taking place in enough universities and colleges in the USA, Canada and Australia in particular to suggest that the new learning technologies could bring about a massive change in post-secondary education and training.**

For instance, whereas previous attempts to use earlier technologies as a replacement for classroom teaching were initiated by technology enthusiasts ('early adopters'), they failed to be used extensively by the main core of university and college teachers. Furthermore, most applications of earlier technologies were either separate and peripheral distance education applications, or were used to enhance classroom teaching, without changing the basic method of classroom organization and teaching.

E-learning though appears to be different. **The reason why distributed learning in particular could be revolutionary is that it requires radical changes to the organization of campus-based teaching.** It raises some fundamental questions, such as:

- on what target groups should e-learning be focused (e.g. high school leavers, students denied access to conventional universities, lifelong learners, international students)?
- how should the mix of face-to-face teaching and e-learning vary, dependent on the target group?
- for what teaching or learning goals should we use face-to-face sessions and for what should we use e-learning?
- what do we need a campus for?
- what kind of space use do we need on campus?

- what instructional and technical support is necessary for e-learning?
- who owns an on-line course?
- what are the training requirements for teaching?
- what technical infrastructure is needed?
- how much will this cost?
- how do we measure the positive and negative effects of e-learning?

Why should governments be involved?

These issues clearly need to be addressed at an institutional level, so why should governments become involved?

The role of the state in managing or regulating post-secondary education and training varies from country to country and even from state to state within federal systems. In many Western countries, governments have traditionally been reluctant to interfere in the day-to-day running of universities, although they have often taken a more direct role in managing colleges. However, since the late 1980s many governments have been increasingly active in regulating, restructuring, and using fiscal policies to influence the behaviour of even large research universities.

In many developing countries, in former communist-bloc countries, in some of the countries with newly emerging advanced economies, and in many southern European countries, governments have always taken a fairly direct role in managing and directing general higher education policy. They define roles (or mandates) for individual institutions, appoint university presidents and/or governing boards, and oversee their budgets and operations at a fairly detailed level. In such countries, post-secondary education and training is often seen as a strategy for national development, and in more authoritarian and less democratic countries, governments have felt the need for direct control of higher education institutions to avoid dissent and counter-revolution.

Technology is presenting some major challenges to the assumptions under which colleges and universities, as well as governments, have operated historically. With ever shortening technology investment cycles, state and institutional planning processes – whether for technology acquisition or programming – have needed streamlining to keep up. Also old conceptions of geographic services areas are challenged in this new networked environment. As the desire to create a more 'market responsive' system grows, so too does the value of a deregulated approach to programme development and oversight.

But there should be no illusions about the 'magic of the marketplace' in providing quality and cost-effective e-learning services and programmes in post-secondary education and training. Some populations and some occupations will be neglected in a 'free market' driven environment. Cost and quality imperatives are driving some institutions together into partnerships and consortia but many others may be slow to realize this self-interest. Risk taking and entrepreneurship in post-secondary education and training are likely to grow, but so too will the need to inform and protect consumers from fraud and abuse.

These dynamics suggest significant new and important roles for governments. Among the new roles being assumed by government in managing technological change in post-secondary education and training are the following:

- deregulator and streamliner of planning and oversight processes;
- stimulator of 'best practice' and 'choice';
- enabler, funder and broker of partnerships;
- creator of 'utilities' or technology networks;
- informer and protector of consumers;
- strategic investor on behalf of the state and its under-served 'customers'.

A government can play a number of strategic roles in the area of technology planning in post-secondary education and training. On the one hand, its academic and financing policies can encourage all institutions to utilize e-learning. On the other hand, it can articulate and operationalize a collective vision for the state post-secondary system with respect to the place and role of e-learning, distributed learning and distance education within the system.

It could be argued that information technology and e-learning planning is most relevant to the following national or statewide priorities:

- the delivery of cost-effective instruction to under-served populations and regions;
- increasing the capacity of all institutions and programmes to utilize the power of technology to carry out their teaching, research, and service functions;
- a more fully articulated system of post-secondary education and training where transitions from one institution and sector to another are enhanced;
- greater capacity of post-secondary education and training institutions to meet the economic development goals of the state and the continuing lifelong learning needs of its citizens;
- a more informed set of consumers about choices and programmes available from state, international and private institutions;
- a better conception of what constitutes best practice in the field of e-learning, distributed learning and distance education;
- a financing, planning, and accountability process that can be used to justify the significant investments of public funds required to achieve these goals.

In this context then, it can be seen that **government has a critically important role to play with respect to planning and managing the development of e-learning in post-secondary education and training.**

Conclusion

Other modern technologies such as satellite TV, compressed video-conferencing, wireless telephony, speech recognition, and machine translation are either already playing an important role in post-secondary education and training or will do so in the near future. However, the main technology driving change in post-secondary education and training is the Internet, and in particular the World Wide Web.

The Web is influencing traditional classroom teaching and the delivery of distance education programmes. However, as stated by a report from the American Council for Education (Oblinger, Barone and Hawkins, 2001), "**distributed learning, rather than distance education, will become the dominant paradigm for higher education**". It is becoming even more critical for corporate training.

These developments will result eventually in radical changes to public-sector institutions. It will require major investment in technology, re-training of post-secondary teachers and trainers, and major reorganization of the institutions. Governments will need to assess the relative roles of the public and private sectors in lifelong learning, and the support needed to encourage the use of e-learning for this purpose.

There are strong instructional reasons for the increased use of the Web in post-secondary education and training. However, **the importance of the Internet for post-secondary education and training is tied closely to social and economic developments.** Successful use of e-learning requires an extensive national technology infrastructure to be in place, and its use is being driven primarily by the needs of knowledge-based economies. Government has an extremely important role to play in planning and managing the development of e-learning in post-secondary education and training, and this booklet attempts to set out some of these critical planning and management issues.

II. What is needed to support e-learning technologies?

Before a plan or strategy can be developed for e-learning in post-secondary education and training, it is important to understand the necessary conditions or requirements for the successful implementation of learning technologies.

The driver of Internet expansion in recent years has clearly been the business community. Very few countries or states have built an Internet technology infrastructure solely for educational or even government purposes, although the original Internet began as an emergency communications network in the USA developed by university researchers.

Nevertheless, government can play a very important role in facilitating the development and expansion of the Internet, and hence increase access and the chances of the Internet being used for post-secondary education and training. In order to identify appropriate roles for government, an understanding of the requirements of e-learning with regard to technology infrastructure is needed, and this in turn requires an understanding of how the Internet works.

How the Internet works

The Internet is a very unusual communications structure. It is basically a network or Web of interconnected computers (servers). Each server is independently owned. As long as it is connected to the Internet and has the necessary software and access codes, any computer can act as a connection within the World Wide Web. Thus everyone's desk-top computer can connect to the Internet, provided it has appropriate software and a connection to an appropriate communications channel. A desk-top computer will send out a coded signal to the host server (in a university, probably located within an academic department or central computing service). The host server will then forward the coded message and 'find' another appropriate server to relay it on, and so on, until it reaches its final destination. If one server is busy, the signal will find another.

Messages are sent in the form of standardized digital data. The data can be transmitted across any communications channel, such as telephone lines, co-axial cable (cable TV), fibre optic cable, satellite transmission, microwave, or wireless.

Sound and pictures can be converted from analog to digital data, or created in digital form, then re-converted at the desk-top back into sound or pictures. Thus all forms of media can be transmitted. However, video requires many times more capacity (bandwidth) than for example text. Not all of analogue television or audio signals need to be sent; the basic picture can be coded, then only changes in the picture transmitted. This is the basis of compressed video or audio. This can considerably reduce the bandwidth required, but can lead to reduction in picture or sound quality (jerkiness in video, staccato or 'clipped' sound). Compression technology though is improving all the time.

The pricing structure is also unusual. The Internet runs on physical networks operated by a wide range of telecommunications organizations, including telephone companies, cable TV companies and satellite operators. However, the service is provided by intermediary companies called Internet Service Providers (ISPs).

Some ISPs may be subsidiaries of telecommunications companies, but basically in a number of countries any organization that can afford to buy telecommunications services in bulk and has the technical knowledge can set itself up as an ISP, including universities. Examples of commercial ISPs are America Online – aol.com – and IBM's hotmail.com. In some emerging Internet markets, the local university can be a major commercial ISP. For instance the public University of Guadalajara is one of the major ISPs in the city of Guadalajara in Mexico. This enables the university to use its research in providing a high quality Internet service, to develop technical expertise in the operation and management of the Internet, to provide a source of employment for graduates, and to use profits to ensure that its own internal Internet network is developed to a high standard.

ISPs buy capacity from different telecommunications providers, and get their money back by charging a monthly Internet service fee from individual consumers. There are various forms of pricing structures, but most are based on a flat rate dependent on bandwidth capacity. This means that once connected and the monthly service charge is paid to the ISP, the user has unlimited access to the Internet, or at a lower rate a restricted number of hours connection per month. Users may also have to pay for the telephone connection. This is increasingly a local call, which in Canada and the USA is usually free (once the monthly service charge to the phone company is paid).

Generally, content providers on the Internet have avoided charging a fee to access their Web sites, although they may recover fees in other ways. For instance, in the case of on-line courses, the content may be free and publicly accessible, but tuition fees may be charged for tutoring and assessment. Other ways content providers make money from the Internet is through advertising on the Web site. Many university and college course sites are password protected and only available once tuition fees have been paid. Commercial sites may also be password protected and may require payment of an annual or monthly subscription fee to access the site.

Reasons for the growth of the Internet

The most amazing thing about the Internet is the speed of connection. Even with a standard telephone line, it is possible to access within a second a site on the other side of the planet (it may take a lot longer to download the Web page, but that is another matter). **Thus once users are connected to the Internet they have almost instant access to all the resources available globally on all the computers connected to the Internet.**

The Internet is enormously flexible. It is independent of any particular communications technology, or any particular computer malfunction within the network. The Internet is not owned or managed by any corporation, government or international organization, although there are international technical bodies that determine technical standards, Web site registration protocols, etc., to ensure inter-connections and security.

Once the network is in place communication costs are low. Internet provision often comes at marginal cost, because it can be added to an already existing system. For instance, universities and colleges usually have an already existing telephone system, and local area computer networks, for administrative purposes.

However, adding Internet capacity usually requires upgrading existing capacity, across all parts of the network, and this is discussed in more detail below. There are also issues of security, pornography, violence, intellectual property, and for some countries national security and subversion around the use of the Internet. These issues though are outside the scope of this monograph.

Institutional networks

The value of a network increases according to the proportion of potential users connected. Thus access to the Internet limited, to say, senior management or to administrative units makes no sense, in that cost of investment in the infrastructure could not be justified by the volume of use. However, many faculty and staff may not have had a computer before or know how to use one.

Thus the major challenge for a university or college is to ensure that all staff and professors have a computer linked to a local area network, which in turn is linked externally to the Internet. It will also be essential to ensure that faculty and staff know how to use computers and have the necessary technical support.

Ensuring that a university or college campus is Internet-ready is no light undertaking. There are several elements to technology infrastructure.

Physical infrastructure

Physical infrastructure includes desktop or laptop machines, mainframes or servers that are linked to desktop machines. It also includes the physical network (cables and wires) that connects all the machines, and the operating software and routers that enable the machines and networks to work. Infrastructure would also include telecommunications links to the world outside the campus, and between campuses, including telephone services, videoconferencing equipment and networks, and of course access to the Internet.

Many universities and colleges have old buildings without adequate conduits for wiring, or asbestos fillings within walls that need to be removed before modern cabling can be installed. An alternative is to use a wireless network, at least for the last few metres of connection. Wireless would for instance allow individual computers within a building to access a network without any physical wiring within the building.

Servers will need to be installed within each department, and/or be networked to other servers on campus. Once networks are installed, equipment and software will need to be continually upgraded because of the rapid rate of technological development in information technologies, which shows no sign of abating.

Internet connections with the outside world will need to be established, and ports and other communications facilities installed to enable students in residences or off-campus to access the main university campus, or satellite campuses and other institutions to be linked.

Large research universities may need to spend up to $4 to $5 million a year to develop and maintain the necessary campus technology infrastructure: high-speed networks that will link every building, and within every building, every classroom and office, and within every classroom and office, every computer workstation.

Human support for infrastructure

Even more important than the physical infrastructure are the people required to make the physical infrastructure work. They may work in a central unit, or may work within a faculty or department to support local technical needs.

There are in fact four levels of human support required to exploit technology to the full. The most obvious level is made up of the technical support people who are needed to ensure that the networks and equipment are properly installed, operated, updated and maintained. These can be described as the *technology infrastructure support staff*.

At the second level are the media production and services staff, such as interface designers, graphics designers, videoconferencing managers, or graduate students who do HTML mark-up. They support the creation and application of educational materials and programmes using technology. These can be described as the *educational technology support staff*. Technology infrastructure staff will be needed whether or not technology is used for teaching; however the educational technology support staff are needed only if or when technology is to be used for teaching.

At the third level are those that provide educational services and expertise, such as instructional design, faculty development, project management, and evaluation, to support the use of technology for teaching. These can be described as the *instructional design* staff.

The fourth level is made up of the professors, instructors, teachers or subject-matter experts, who create content and provide the teaching over the networks and infrastructure. These can be described as the *subject experts*.

While the latter two groups are not critical elements of the technology infrastructure, they are essential for the creation and delivery of high quality technology-based teaching.

Funding infrastructure

Governments often treat large-scale investment in physical facilities and equipment as a *capital* investment, i.e. a one-off cost, although institutions may need to pay annual interest payments and allow for depreciation. An institution with no, little, or very out-of-date existing technology infrastructure may indeed initially require a heavy one-time investment, but **in general, technology infrastructure requires regular ongoing funding**, for two reasons. First, the technology changes very rapidly due to technical advances. For instance, the average life of a desktop computer is three years or so, as the power and functionality of computers constantly develops. Secondly, the cost of human support for the infrastructure usually far exceeds the cost of equipment replacement and upgrading. Thus, **investment in technological infrastructure** within and between institutions **should be seen as a recurrent or *operational* cost.**

When physical infrastructure is treated as a capital expenditure, it is less likely to compete for funds that impact directly on teaching. However, as an operational cost, the need to fund technology support staff directly competes with funds for teaching and research. Consequently, **the human technology support side is often underfunded in many educational institutions.**

This may explain why the most consistent complaint across universities and colleges from those responsible for technology applications is the inadequacy of resources for human technical support for technology.

Further down the chain, from technological support to educational technology support, it becomes even more difficult to secure adequate resources. If the network crashes, its impact is obvious; the value of an instructional designer is much harder to justify when funds are tight. Nevertheless, from a teaching and learning perspective, it is critical that academics and instructors receive the training and educational support needed.

Lastly, the most expensive link in the chain is the subject expert. Without their time and energy there will be no teaching or educational materials developed and distributed across the infrastructure.

It is essential of course to have a strategy for developing the technology infrastructure of a university. Priorities must be set on both the level of investment and the areas of investment. In particular, the right balance has to be struck between capital and recurring costs, and between physical infrastructure and human support.

From a central government perspective, it needs to be recognized that most public post-secondary institutions will not be able to afford the high investment and operational costs needed to support the use of e-learning within previous funding levels, without severely cutting other services. The investment in technical equipment and upgrading alone is likely to increase operating costs by around 2-5 per cent per annum.

More of a challenge for many countries will be finding sufficient numbers of qualified technical staff to support the institutional technical infrastructure, as such staff are scarce and can usually earn good salaries in the private sector. Thus **the total cost of building an efficient, comprehensive technical infrastructure and fully staffing it is likely to add another 10 per cent to most institutions' annual operating costs.**

Will not such an investment lead to savings in other areas, such as fewer teachers? This is unlikely in the short term. Teachers also need to learn not only how to use the technology, but more importantly how to reorganize their teaching, in order to exploit fully the benefits of e-learning. This takes time and is a cost to the institution. Secondly, probably **the most important instructional benefit of the Internet is to increase flexible interaction between teachers and students. If technology is used to replace teachers, then this benefit is lost.** As with business, the **main benefit of the investment in technology is not so much to reduce costs as to gain competitive advantage.** This is achieved by using the technology to improve the quality of learning and to develop learners who are better prepared for a knowledge-based society.

Implications for government planning

In order to access the Internet, there are four requirements for users:

- an appropriate computer with the required software;
- a connection to a telecommunications carrier;
- an Internet Service Provider;
- the ability to pay for services.

The main barrier to using the Internet for education and training purposes is that many students cannot access the Internet or, even if they could, they do not have the necessary equipment or funds to purchase the equipment. **Governments have a critical role to play in widening access to the Internet.**

In theory, the Internet could operate under any system of government regulation. Thus a nationally owned telecommunications monopoly could be mandated by the government to provide Internet services. Governments could build their own telecommunications networks for education and other government services.

However, the rapid expansion, high quality and low cost of the Internet have been driven mainly by competition and the controlled deregulation of telecommunications services.

To keep down prices to consumers, telecommunications carriers must be required by government regulation to open up their services to independent ISPs. Internet Service Providers need to be relatively independent of the telecommunications carriers, and have alternative carriers with which to connect, so they can shop around for the best price. End users must have alternative Internet Service Providers, to ensure quality of service.

This is one reason why there is relative diversity in the cost of access to the Internet between different countries, and hence in the number or proportion of users connected to the Internet. **There is strong evidence that both the expansion of Internet infrastructure and the proportion of users of the Internet are closely related to commercially competitive regulatory environments.**

It is much more expensive for a telecommunications carrier to provide services to sparsely populated areas than to high-density areas, and to 'light' users compared with 'heavy' users. Thus, in a completely free market, telecommunications carriers will differentially price connections in low-density and high-density areas, and for low-volume and high-volume users. Consequently, a business in a downtown city skyscraper would be charged much less for telephone or Internet connections and service than a farmer in a remote mountainous region. Thus **an unregulated free market will result in higher costs for poorer people, and hence loss of service.**

There are various strategies government can adopt to ensure more equal access to telecommunications services and hence the Internet. One simple measure is to require carriers to provide the same service at the same price, irrespective of location or type of user. Thus a telecommunications carrier would average its costs between low-cost and high-cost users.

Another measure is for the government to use its clout as a major 'corporate' client. Government agencies such as hospitals, schools, and government offices can constitute a large component of a telecommunications company's business. By 'bulk buying' services from one carrier in a competitive market, government can drive down the cost of telecommunications. More importantly, by issuing a 'request for proposal' (rfp) that states pre-determined requirements, such as connection to previously un-served schools or colleges as part of the deal, governments can increase telecommunications and hence Internet access to more remote areas. The contract would go to the carrier (or consortium of carriers) offering the best range of services, combining price with connectivity and service. Alternatively, governments may pay the extra cost of connecting remote sites such as schools or community centres, although this is likely to be a more expensive strategy than issuing an rfp.

A third strategy is for government to build its own educational or government network, either as the sole telecommunications carrier, or in direct competition or even partnership with existing carriers. This might be used as a last resort if the private-sector telecommunications companies are not meeting government expectations regarding the development of accessible Internet services. The Government of Malaysia has created an extensive fibre optic 'corridor' between the city centre of the capital, Kuala Lumpur, and the international airport. Its aim is to encourage the development of high-tech companies along the corridor, and the development of advanced Internet services, as part of a push to become a major 'knowledge-based' economy. In the USA, several state governments, such as Kentucky and Indiana, have built their own educational telecommunications networks, in areas where traffic is comparatively less dense and competition from telecommunications carriers is less intense.

In order to widen Internet access, a number of countries have developed strategies for local community access to the Internet. Naidoo (2001) has described a number of such initiatives. These include community learning centres, telecentres in schools or business locations, and Internet or cybercafés. The government's role can be direct, such as funding the equipment, connectivity and operation of local community centres; or indirect, by providing free or reduced price Internet connections, or tax breaks to commercial organizations.

Lastly, taxation and student-grant policies can be used to encourage increased access and use of the Internet. Students who need to purchase a computer or need an ISP account in order to study might be allowed to claim at least part of the cost against their income tax, or be given a grant or repayable loan for this purpose. Those building the infrastructure may be given tax incentives to bring services to poor city neighbourhoods or more remote areas.

However, in general, **most governments will be content to leave the development of infrastructure to the private sector, within a general government policy framework that encourages access and affordability to all citizens.**

Sometimes major corporations will approach government for a partnership arrangement to increase Internet access or to provide computer equipment for schools. While this can bring benefits in the form of lower prices, technical support services, and standardization of equipment, governments need to be very careful in tying themselves too tightly to a single supplier of services. The technology is undergoing rapid change, and it could be dangerous to be committed for more than three years to any particular technology solution. Often 'partnership' proposals from the private sector are no more than a subtle marketing device. More importantly, government is often too far removed from the application of technology in the classroom or workplace to judge the implications of tying the institutions to a particular supplier, so it is best to leave these decisions at a local level. **In a period of rapid development, there is much to be said for a diversity of approaches to technology investment within a whole national system.**

In many countries, of course, the policy framework for the development and regulation of telecommunications services is likely to rest with Ministries of Industry or Communications, rather than Education. However, if a country's national policy is to develop the growth of a knowledge-based economy, then the Ministry of Education needs to work closely with the Ministry responsible for government policy and regulation in the telecommunications area. Indeed, **several of the more economically advanced countries are now developing a national e-learning strategy as part of a broader national skills and training policy** encompassing several different government Ministries and departments.

Conclusions

Whatever strategies governments choose to adopt themselves or leave to the private sector, it needs to be recognized that **the effective use of e-learning for education and training purposes is absolutely dependent on a widely accessible and low-cost national telecommunications infrastructure.** It also needs to be recognized that government policy can immensely facilitate or hinder the growth of the Internet for educational use.

In summary, then, **government can certainly develop policies that will encourage a rapid growth of the Internet**, as follows:

- controlled deregulation of telecommunications services,;
- encouraging competition between telecommunications suppliers;
- bulk buying of government telecommunications services through competitive bidding from suppliers;
- careful regulation to ensure access to all (e.g. by making it a condition of licensing that user fees are averaged between urban and rural clients);
- tax breaks to infrastructure suppliers to incite investment and/or tax breaks on computers and Internet services to end users, thus encouraging greater use;
- open and corruption-free licensing practices to encourage genuine competition;

- developing a national strategy for e-learning and e-commerce that seeks to co-ordinate activities across different government departments.

III. Building on the existing public sector post-secondary education infrastructure

There are several different strategies that can be adopted by government to encourage the growth of e-learning. The choice of strategies will to some extent depend on political ideologies, the current pressing education and training needs, and the current status of post-secondary education and training within any particular country. There is an element of risk and a range of possible dangers as well as benefits in each of these strategies. Strategies for e-learning need to be embedded within a wider framework of government policy for economic and social development.

In this chapter the focus is on developing strategies within the existing public-sector post-secondary system. The next chapter will look at some more radical approaches that to some extent bypass existing institutions. The following chapters will then look at the costs of e-learning and the implications for funding strategies.

There is much that national or state governments can do to facilitate the development of e-learning within existing public post-secondary institutions. In the long run, this is likely to be the most sustainable policy with the biggest impact, although it will require additional and significant public-sector investment.

Regulation

The traditional means by which governments have tried to ensure quality of provision of higher education is through the accreditation of institutions; in other words, licensing institutions to award nationally recognized qualifications such as degrees, diplomas and certificates.

However, **e-learning recognizes no national boundaries.** A student can log on from home in any country and access a course or programme from an institution in another country, provided they have Internet access and the necessary money to pay for the service. The student can do this with or without the blessing of his or her government. Thus trying to stop foreign institutions from offering programmes into a country by refusing them accreditation is a fairly futile operation. Welcome to globalization.

However, this does not mean that governments should do nothing. Perhaps the most important role is to educate consumers, either through developing guidelines and a set of questions for students to ask before enrolling for on-line programmes, or by using guidelines developed elsewhere. This is discussed in more detail in the next chapter (see Hope, 2001, Institute for Higher Education Policy, 2001, and the Quality Assurance Agency for Higher Education, 1999, for more discussion of quality assurance for e-learning in higher education).

Governments can certainly play an important role in regulating on-line programmes from institutions within their own country. **E-learning programmes should be subjected to the same process of accreditation as any other programme.** It does not need to be stricter than the accreditation of on-campus programmes, but it is important to ensure that the specific requirements of on-line programmes, such as access to (on-line) library facilities and appropriate on-line tutoring, are adequately met.

If governments have confidence in their public-sector institutions to properly ensure the quality of their own on-line programmes, no further regulation is needed than the normal degree approval procedure. Some jurisdictions have a government-appointed commission or committee that licenses private schools, colleges and universities within the country, and the role of regulating on-line programmes by such institutions could be included in their mandate.

The difficulty lies with programmes coming from institutions located outside the country. Again, many countries have a process for recognizing qualifications from abroad, either done through a central government organization, or delegated to individual national universities and colleges. This process could also be used for accrediting students who have taken on-line programmes from a foreign institution.

However, in some ways this is too late. Students who in good faith have taken a course from an institution that has not been previously accredited may suffer. There may then be a value in requiring foreign institutions to be accredited by the appropriate national body or institutions, and warning students to ensure that the courses they propose to take from a foreign organization will be recognized by such an accreditation body.

Another mechanism that can ensure foreign e-learning programmes meet national accreditation standards and cultural requirements is through partnership of a recognized national institution with a foreign provider. Thus governments could encourage partnerships with carefully selected, reputable foreign universities, colleges and appropriate private-sector institutions for the delivery of on-line learning.

Competition

In a 'free market' ideology, governments give institutions complete freedom to compete with one another. Institutions are judged against government-agreed performance criteria and are funded accordingly, or are allowed to collect more and more of their revenues through student or client fees. In a truly competitive market, the strong institutions survive, and the weak die. Governments may not worry too much then about e-learning competition from organizations in other countries, if it leads to better standards for local students and forces local institutions to improve.

It could be argued that in a newly emerging technological environment, such as e-learning, the best policy is to let a thousand flowers bloom. This will encourage innovation, and competition between institutions will spur more rapid developments, and will automatically weed out inappropriate developments.

Government's role then in planning and managing e-learning in a free-market policy framework is minimal once national standards have been set and performance measures put in place. Infrastructure development will be left to the private sector, and institutions will have the freedom individually to decide the extent to which they wish to engage in e-learning. The market will determine who is right.

One can see this as a possible strategy in a country where there are already at least some strong local institutions and an extensive Internet infrastructure with wide access. It is difficult however to see how a 'pure' free-market framework could work where the infrastructure is lacking and where institutions do not currently have the technical capacity or academic reputation to compete on a global basis. Such a policy approach is bound to widen inequalities in access and to place many institutions at a competitive disadvantage.

Without however an alternative or specific government policy or framework for e-learning, this is the default mode: institutions will start competing with each other for students and resources. Some of the dangers of this can be seen if we look at role and mission issues.

Role and mission issues

One of the most important functions of government has been to establish or negotiate an effective division of roles and responsibilities, at the broadest mission level, among post-secondary institutions.

In the two-year college sector, the focus may for instance be on vocational training and preparation, high school certification and completion for those who did not graduate from high school, language training for immigrants, and basic adult education. Colleges have traditionally focused on their immediate geographical location, providing a community-based service.

Within the university sector, there may be differentiation between university colleges that offer no more than bachelor's degrees, comprehensive universities that provide a range of undergraduate and graduate programmes and research, and a smaller number of elite and advanced research universities. In some countries, there is a single, most prestigious national university, where resources are channelled to enable it to compete internationally in specific areas, and other more local universities and colleges distributed across the nation, sometimes affiliated with or supervised by the national university.

The private sector may focus on work-related and company-based training, and may by regulation be prevented from awarding nationally recognized accreditation, or may be allowed to offer accreditation in specifically vocational areas.

This approach to market differentiation in post-secondary education and training tends to maximize public and employer support, minimize institutional conflict, and focus individual institutions on distinctive niches. E-learning however tends to disrupt such neat arrangements. **One of the consequences of the spread of e-learning is that it calls into question the mission of different institutions**, especially those with a regional or geographical remit.

The apparent transparency of easy-to-use technologies such as the World Wide Web, and the development of alternative distribution networks, make it easier and easier for individual faculty members and programmes to gain at least an entry foothold in a global learning market. A college may develop a course for its own students but also be able to offer it nationally or internationally.

What happens though if several institutions within a state, for instance, develop the same degree programme for which there is a limited local market? Governments may become concerned at seeming duplication of services within its jurisdiction, or at the funding of programmes that are taken mainly by out-of-state students. Sooner or later politicians and policy-makers will be asking why they are funding multiple versions of the same course from several different institutions, when students anywhere in the state could take just one. Government, for instance, may question why a particular university wants to launch a global on-line MBA when two existing universities are already struggling to compete in this market against strong foreign competition, and when other specifically local business education needs are not being met. Thus, **the development of e-learning can lead to unnecessary duplication of effort.**

While it is certainly possible for any given faculty member or institution to launch an Internet-based course 'to the world,' it is far more questionable whether these individual initiatives can sustain themselves over the long term. For instance, what is the competitive advantage of the institution on a global basis? E-learning programmes need considerable up-front investment. If such ventures fail, and if this occurs on a large scale across a system, government quite rightly will be concerned about the waste of public resources.

The internationalization of on-line learning will depend on competitive advantage, of having unique programmes delivered at an appropriate price and quality. Governments may want to encourage different centres of academic or research excellence in different institutions, to ensure the development of programming for different market niches, based on local or national needs, and the mission and mandate of a particular institution. They may want to focus e-learning developments in their strongest universities and colleges, or alternatively they may want to strengthen otherwise weak or vulnerable institutions through new e-learning developments.

With regard to e-learning, it is critical for institutional missions to be defined in terms of whether an institution's student focus is primarily local, national or international. Many of these decisions will need to be made at a local level by the academic departments and institutions themselves, but **government can help avoid waste and duplication by providing an enabling policy framework built around institutional mission and role, and institutional strengths.**

One way a government can develop such a policy framework for e-learning, strengthening institutions' international competitiveness, and reducing unnecessary duplication, is through a co-operative policy symposium. This would provide an opportunity for these issues to be discussed by government and the various institutional stakeholders, and to develop a policy document based on consensus or government leadership. For the results of such an approach, see the Government of British Columbia's (2000) policy framework for educational technology: http://www.aved.gov.bc.ca/strategic/edtech/execsum/execsum.pdf

Partnerships

Partnerships and consortia may be set up for a variety of reasons, but three of the most important are to share costs (or spread the same cost over greater numbers of students), to fight off perceived competition for students from other sources, and to avoid unnecessary duplication within the system.

We shall see in the next chapter that e-learning requires up-front fixed costs which are independent of student numbers (e.g. creating a Web site). If these costs can be shared across a larger number of students, or if two institutions can share the costs and use the same materials, then there are possibilities of economies of scale through institutions working together. In addition, one institution may have more knowledge, resources or experience in the area, and partnership provides both an immediate access to e-learning for the partner with less experience, and an opportunity to develop its own skills and resources through working with its more experienced partner.

Tec de Monterrey in Mexico has had a very successful partnership with the University of British Columbia in Canada. UBC developed five on-line courses that were integrated with Tec de Monterrey's own on-line Master's in Educational Technology. Tec de Monterrey initially paid UBC half the cost of developing the five courses. Tec de Monterrey had the rights to offer the programme in Latin America. UBC had the rights to offer its five courses elsewhere in the world. After five years, the two institutions have decided to enter into a full and equal partnership. They will offer a joint Master's in Educational Technology, available both in Spanish and English, on a global basis, with faculty from both institutions working together on courses, and also developing courses in their own language.

It should be noted that this partnership was developed without any government assistance, on a fully cost-recoverable basis. However, Tec de Monterrey is a private university, and the fee levels, at US$8,000, will price many students out of the market. As a consequence the Mexican Federal Government is supporting the programme with 120 scholarships per year for Mexican teachers. Governments could do a great deal to foster partnerships of this kind and at the same time help keep costs down to students by scholarships or subsidy. This may still be cheaper and more effective than individual institutions trying to build their own e-learning programmes from scratch.

Such partnerships can also act as a means of entry into the global e-learning market for less economically advanced countries. The partner institution from the less economically developed country brings adaptation to local culture, language benefits, local or national accreditation, sharing of costs and risks, and access to neighbouring markets or markets with similar language and culture. These are all considerable benefits for the partner from the more developed country.

Consortia

Consortia involve more than two institutions in a formal collaborative arrangement. Many state systems already have provision for transfer of credit for courses or whole programmes between colleges and universities. Students qualifying from a two-year college may then transfer into the third year of a university programme. Credit or programme transfer is much enhanced through e-learning, as the students may be able to take the third and fourth year university courses at a distance, without moving from their community. To show the roles that government can play in facilitating consortia based on distance education, three examples from North America are given.

The Open University of British Columbia (Canada)

Three public universities (University of British Columbia, University of Victoria, and Simon Fraser University), and the Open Learning Agency (OLA) in British Columbia, have operated a very successful collaborative system since 1979. (The province of British Columbia is responsible for post-secondary education). There are a number of elements to this consortium:

- open access for students; no prior qualifications are required to register with the Open Learning Agency;

- students can combine distance courses from the three universities and OLA, irrespective of prior qualifications, or by transferring approved two-year college programmes (usually taken in the conventional manner) into a two year third and fourth year university degree programme, taken at a distance, to acquire a fully distance degree;

- students who take a degree this way are awarded a degree from the Open University of British Columbia through the Open Learning Agency (http://www.ola.bc.ca/bcou/home.html), and the degree is recognized by government and the Association of Universities and Colleges of Canada. There have been over 1,100 graduates from this programme;

- students can also transfer credits from one institution to another, so that a student admitted to UBC (through the usual selective process) can take, for example, a distance education course from the University of Victoria or the Open Learning Agency and transfer it into his or her own UBC programme;

- joint planning to avoid duplication of courses: the universities and OLA meet on a regular basis to exchange programme information and to avoid duplication of distance education programmes as far as possible; this operates on a voluntary basis;

- joint publicity and marketing of distance education courses and programmes at university level; OLA publishes a single calendar and now a Web site that lists all the courses and programmes available by distance within the province at university level;

- OLA also provides free student counselling and advisory services for anyone wanting to take a university-level distance education course or programme; the universities provide a similar service for their own students or external students wanting to take or transfer distance courses to or from their own institution;

- OLA operates a 'credit bank', whereby students with qualifications from outside the province or state can have these accredited for use within the province, enabling them to transfer these credits into other partner institutions' programmes.

The system has worked for so long and so well for several reasons. Government funding is based on a fixed amount per full time equivalent enrolment (FTE) at a particular institution. Irrespective of where the student finally graduates or even registers, the institution offering a particular course gets the equivalent FTE funding for each course enrolment.

Secondly, the government funded the Open University operation of the Open Learning Agency, and originally included funds for distance education with the general operating grant for each of the three universities. Also, until recently the government put a small amount of money each year (C$500,000) into the consortium for new programme development. Most of this was used for course development by the three universities, and the rest for the course calendar and student advice in distance education programmes by OLA. While the $500,000 was only a small proportion of what each institution put into distance education, it brought people to the table. Although this funding has now been withdrawn, the universities and OLA have agreed to continue to collaborate with regard to programming.

Thus, a third reason is the willingness of the institutional leadership consistently to work collaboratively rather than in competition with each other within the province, which is perhaps the most unusual and important feature of the consortium.

Lastly, through an Act in the provincial legislature the government created a co-ordinating agency (OLA) with a mandate to widen access through collaboration with existing institutions, and the power to award degrees.

The Western Governors' University (United States of America)

The Western Governors' University (WGU) (http://www.wgu.edu/wgu/index.html) opened officially in June, 1998. In August, 2001 it had governors from 19 member states as Board members. It had 19 leading business partners, including America Online, Apple, AT&T, Cisco, IBM, KPMG, Microsoft, Novell and Sun. It had 37 participating educational institutions, including some well-known state universities and colleges, such as Brigham Young, Northern Arizona University, and Texas Tech, as well as private-sector course providers.

WGU is based on the concept of *competency-based learning*, and the business partners are important because they help to determine the competences required. WGU has no faculty, it does not plan to develop its own courses, and it has rejected the concept of credit hours or 'time spent' studying as the basis for degree accreditation.

Students can achieve their qualifications in two ways. The most innovative is by demonstrating set standards of competency through successful completion of tests and assessment, irrespective of prior courses taken. Students will however be advised as to which courses in the WGU catalogue will help them reach these competencies through a personalized 'Academic Action Plan' (AAP).

WGU's 'recognized' courses that produce the requisite competences are delivered by distance, mainly through e-learning, and come from other providers, such as universities, colleges and the private sector. WGU 'brokers' and validates these courses.

The Electronic Campus (United States of America)

The Southern Regional Education Board (SREB), which created the Electronic Campus, is governed by a board that consists of the governor of each member state and four people that he or she appoints, including at least one state legislator and at least one educator. SREB is supported by appropriations from its member states and by funds from private companies, foundations, and state and federal agencies.

The Southern Regional Education Board's Electronic Campus describes itself as a *marketplace* for on-line college and university courses from almost 300 college and university campuses across 16 southern states in the USA. Students can:

- identify programmes and courses that are available electronically;
- search by college or university, discipline, level and state for more detailed information, including course descriptions and how the programmes and courses are delivered;
- connect directly to the college or university that offers a chosen course to learn about registration, enrolment and cost;
- pay tuition fees at the same rate across all the programmes offered.

However the Electronic Campus, unlike the Open University of British Columbia and the Western Governors' University, does not award credentials. Students still have to enrol directly with a particular institution offering a course, and individual institutions still negotiate credit transfer arrangements on a case-by-case basis (go to http://www.electroniccampus.org/ for more information).

The role of government in facilitating e-learning consortia

In the first example, the provincial government of British Columbia created the Open Learning Agency and the Open University degree programme through an Act of the legislature. It funded the Open Learning Agency on an annual basis, and for many years provided a relatively small amount of money to bring the other partners to the table to collaborate.

In the second, WGU was created because of the founding governors' frustration that existing universities and colleges were not responding to the needs of business and industry, were not preparing students properly for the new world of work, and were not being flexible enough in recognizing prior learning experiences in non-academic settings.

The Electronic Campus is a looser form of collaboration, bringing together into one Web site, mainly for publicity and information purposes, a very wide range of programmes available to students in the region.

These examples have been given to show some of the creative roles that government can play in creating new institutions, facilitating collaboration, and ensuring that e-learning is widely accessible to as many of its citizens as possible.

A number of lessons can be learned from the experiences of these different consortia arrangements. In particular, the strength of a consortium can be measured by answers to the following questions:

1. Can a potential student take a whole programme through the consortium without having to physically move between institutions?

2. Can a student automatically or without too much trouble transfer credits and courses from one institution to another within the consortium?

3. Does the consortium provide 'one-stop shopping', namely student services (advice, counselling, and tutoring), registration for any institution in the consortium, fee payment, at any single point?

4. Do students have a much wider range of choice of courses, and at a better quality, resulting from the consortium's activities?

5. Is there consistency in fees between courses and programmes offered by the various consortium partners? In other words, can a student pay the same fee for the same kind of course, irrespective of which consortium partner it comes from?

For consortia to work, the members really need to be of roughly the same status, so that there are no barriers to credit transfer, to movement of students between member institutions, and to acceptance of common academic standards between the member institutions.

While both Western Governors' University and the Electronic Campus are mainly dependent on on-line courses, collaborative arrangements of this kind can work with any form of distance education, as the Open University of B.C. example has shown. Technology is not a particularly important condition for consortia to work. Educational, administrative and political conditions are more significant. However, **technology, and particularly the threat from out-of-state e-learning programmes, can provide the incentive to bring institutions together to collaborate.**

International consortia

A number of public and private universities have formed consortia and partnerships with the private sector to exploit commercially their e-learning initiatives. (For a good discussion of this issue, see Dirr, 2001.)

Universitas 21 is a network of 17 universities in mainly Commonwealth countries, including Nottingham University, University of Glasgow, University of Melbourne, Hong Kong University, National University of Singapore and the University of British Columbia. Thomson Publishing and Universitas 21 have announced a partnership to found an 'e-university'.

The universities have a somewhat curious role in this partnership, mainly providing a 50 per cent share of the financing with Thomson Publishing, and supervising quality control through a jointly owned spin-off company. Thomson Publishing will do course development and delivery, buying content on a contract basis from multiple sources, and most likely drawing on its own archive of publications as sources of content.

UNext, a US company, has established an e-university called Cardean (http://www.cardean.com/cgi-bin/cardean1/view/public_home.jsp) that adapts its teaching material from that of the universities of Columbia, Stanford, Chicago, Carnegie Mellon, and the London School of Economics. Degrees are awarded under the Cardean name, endorsed by the State of Illinois.

NextEd Limited (www.nexted.com) is an education and training infrastructure company that partners with universities and professional education providers to market and deliver their courses over the Internet to students and organizations based in Asia. NextEd's focus is on the delivery of accredited higher education and professional certification training to the adult continuous learner market.

Headquartered in Hong Kong with operations in Australia, the People's Republic of China, and the United States of America, NextEd's services include the conversion, hosting and delivery of courses over a dedicated pan-Asian server network, and student marketing and support throughout the Asia-Pacific region. Programmes available on-line from NextEd client universities include courses in business administration, education, nursing, and continuing legal and medical education.

Founded in October 1998, NextEd has agreements with 12 universities located in Australia, Canada, Holland, New Zealand, the United Kingdom and the United States of America. These include the

Universities of Glamorgan and Derby in the United Kingdom, Athabasca University in Canada, La Trobe and the University of Southern Queensland in Australia, the Open Polytechnic and the Auckland University of Technology in New Zealand, and the University of Wisconsin Milwaukee and George Washington University in the United States of America. As of April 2000, over 2,600 students from 21 countries were enrolled in 200 courses hosted by NextEd. The target market of NextEd is the Asian higher education market with an annual value of US$50 billion. Of this, some US$6 billion is spent annually in distance education programmes by roughly 4.2 million students in Asia, according to NextEd.

There is much uncertainty about the business models being adopted by these initiatives, and even more uncertainty about the quality of the education being provided this way. However, a great deal of money is being invested in global e-learning initiatives, and it will be surprising if a powerful global e-learning business does not eventually emerge, probably with private and publicly funded universities as part of the business partnerships. Such businesses will eventually directly compete with less well-funded public universities and colleges, and governments will need to be clear as to what their strategies and policies will be in such a situation. Governments need also to consider the policy implications of publicly funded higher education institutions' partnerships with the private sector, an issue that will be discussed more fully in the last chapter.

Benefits of consortia

In a consortium model, different institutions share common resources as far as possible (such as marketing, electronic and human networks, distance education expertise, and learning centres), and agree among themselves to avoid duplication and to work together wherever possible on joint course development and delivery. Students are able to take courses from different institutions within the consortium and transfer credit as appropriate. Sometimes the consortium itself will award the accreditation, rather than the individual institutions.

Building and strengthening a collaborative approach between institutions has the advantage of avoiding duplication and accessing a higher level of infrastructure and resource than would otherwise be possible. More importantly, it enables institutions to learn and grow from the experience of working together and to leverage important qualitative improvements and economies of scale. Lastly, **a well-organized national consortium with a comprehensive range of e-learning programmes provides a powerful alternative choice for students considering out-of-state and private-sector e-learning providers.**

However, successful consortia are difficult to set up. A successful consortium requires a lot of hard work to develop and sustain. Successful consortia need funding mechanisms that reward and facilitate collaboration. They need institutions to be of roughly equal status. Most of all they need a change of culture within organizations, from one of fierce competitiveness between institutions to one of trust and goodwill between the partner organizations. It is for this reason more than any other that there are few really successful e-learning consortia in the world today.

Conclusion

E-learning will increasingly challenge the traditional means of governing and regulating public post-secondary education systems. **Governments will not be able to build a wall round their country to protect themselves from the influence of foreign e-learning providers.** Even if a country is not ready or willing to develop its own e-learning programmes, it cannot avoid the national issues raised by e-learning. The barbarians are at the gates, if not already inside them.

This does not mean that governments are powerless to influence events. Probably **the most effective strategy in the long run will be to meet competition from outside head-on by building strong internal e-learning programmes through the existing public sector.** This may mean focusing efforts initially on one or two nationally prestigious or innovative institutions (this is discussed in more detail in the next chapter).

However, especially for small or economically less developed countries, competition between local institutions in the field of e-learning is likely to be counter-productive. The real competition for local universities and colleges will come from outside the system, from foreign universities and from the private sector. The resources and skills in economically less well developed countries are likely to be too scarce to enable lots of programmes from different institutions to be developed to a quality that can compete with those coming from outside. Thus, for instance, **small states in a region** such as the South Pacific or Caribbean **would probably benefit a great deal from building a strong e-learning consortium or a single regional e-learning institution.**

Globalization is beginning to lead to international consortia and partnerships, as universities, like media organizations, try to protect their future through strategic alliances, global positioning, and new markets. Increasingly governments will need to determine what role they should play in encouraging or regulating their own institutions in such partnerships and consortia.

Governments can do much also to lever economies of scale, and concentrate scarce skills in developing and running e-learning programmes, by encouraging or building strong national consortia. For a national collaborative e-learning system to work, however, there will in most cases need to be a major shift in the culture of the institutions themselves. Collaboration requires a major change of attitude from a large number of existing staff, especially university and college Presidents, Rectors or Vice-Chancellors, who are accustomed to competing with each other for scarce resources. Leadership from government can help in the form of a structure or mechanisms to encourage collaboration, as well as appropriate financial incentives. Governments themselves can provide leadership by collaborating with other regional governments with regard to e-learning.

Lastly, **governments can prepare themselves and their institutions by an inclusive process of discussion and policy development with the key stakeholders.** E-learning raises some fundamental issues regarding national policy for post-secondary education and training, some of which are discussed in the last chapter. Government can encourage the development of policy forums on the role of e-learning within the public post-secondary education and training system with all key stakeholders, and these forums could be used to help clarify government and institutional polices towards e-learning.

IV. Alternative national e-learning strategies

There are several strategies that can be adopted by government to encourage the growth of e-learning, besides or as well as supporting the development of e-learning in existing public-sector institutions. These can be summarized as follows:

1. Create new e-learning institutions.
2. Encourage private-sector and international providers to develop e-learning for post-secondary education and training.
3. Use e-learning as a means to transform post-secondary education to make it more cost-effective, more learner-centred and more economically relevant.
4. Develop or facilitate a national e-learning business sector.
5. Develop or facilitate a national archive of e-learning materials.
6. Do nothing.

Create a national e-university or e-college

Governments can provide leadership in new areas of development by creating new institutions. An excellent example of this in the field of post-secondary education and training was the creation of the Open University in the United Kingdom in 1969 by the Prime Minister of the time, Harold Wilson. There are useful lessons from the creation of open universities that can be applied to the development of e-learning.

The British Open University was created to expand university-level education for working adults. At the time, British universities served only a small proportion of those leaving high school, and as a result there was a pent-up demand from adults denied access to university. Wilson's model was based on the use of the most advanced technologies of the day, the mass communications technologies of broadcasting (television and radio) and print. The Open University now serves over 160,000 students a year, and it has been the model for other similar institutions in many other countries (see for instance Perry, 1970; Rumble and Harry, 1982; and Daniel, 1998, for descriptions of open universities).

It is perhaps not surprising then that over 30 years later, David Blunkett, the British Minister of Education, announced in 2001 the creation of a national e-university, based on e-learning. Its aim, according to its Web site (http://www.hefce.ac.uk/Pubs/CircLets/2000/cl04_00a.htm), is "to establish a globally competitive provider of higher education programmes through virtual distance learning."

"It will not develop its own programmes on traditional lines using its own staff. Rather, it will work with universities, colleges and other partners to identify and make available a planned portfolio of higher education programmes, learning materials and support services to meet, in an academically coherent way, market demand for e-learning overseas and in the United Kingdom" (http://www.hefce.ac.uk/pubs/hefce/2000/00_43.htm).

Thus the British e-university is planned to work closely with, and facilitate, on-line learning in existing universities and colleges in the United Kingdom.

Kim Beazley, the leader of the opposition Australian Labour Party, made a somewhat similar announcement around the same time. (http://www.alp.org.au/media/0101/kbspuao240101.html).

There are several advantages in creating a national e-university or e-college:

- it allows a country to concentrate scarce high-quality technical and educational staff in a single operation;
- it enables the country to focus the efforts of the e-university or e-college on pressing workforce or educational training needs;
- it helps exploit and develop the existing Internet technology infrastructure;
- it provides a model for existing institutions of the advantages and benefits of e-learning;
- it provides a national alternative to imported e-learning programmes from other countries;
- it could export programmes on a regional or language basis and possibly recover some of its costs in this way.

Experience, however, from the creation of open universities around the world suggests the following conditions for success:

- easy and affordable access to the chosen technology by those students at whom the initiative is targeted;
- strong political leadership at the highest level; in a democracy such an initiative will require at least tacit support from opposition as well as governing parties, to ensure continuity when governments change;
- it must meet a national education or training need that is not being met well in other ways;
- substantial and continuous funding, in the order of several million dollars a year at a minimum;
- academic credibility, either through the award of nationally recognized credentials by the institution itself, or through the ability to transfer accreditation to other nationally recognized institutions;
- good-quality learner support, in the form of efficient administration, student interaction with subject experts, and educational mentoring;
- at least tacit acceptance, and preferably support and assistance, from existing national higher education institutions.

It is critical that the technology is available to those students at whom the institution is targeted. For instance, the new institution might work with existing universities or colleges to provide programmes in the areas where these institutions themselves do not have sufficient resources to offer programmes, such as in information technology, e-commerce, or biotechnology. The participating institutions would provide the necessary technological support on their campuses for the new institution's students. Alternatively, the government may choose to invest in selected local learning centres, such as schools or colleges, where the equipment could be shared by both the local institution and the e-university or e-college.

It may be wondered why existing open universities could also not be mandated to develop e-learning programmes, rather than develop yet another institution. However, the primary mandate of open universities is to widen access. If many potential students do not have access to a computer or the Internet, focusing on e-learning will divert open universities away from their primary mission. Nevertheless, there may be specific target groups or programmes where open universities could develop on-line learning. For instance the Indira Gandhi National Open University in India has developed on-line programmes in computer science and management (see Sharma, 2001, for more details).

For countries with limited resources for e-learning, concentrating them in a single national resource could be a very useful first step in developing a national e-learning strategy. A new e-university or e-college will be particularly useful if it is based on sharing equipment and new initiatives with existing institutions, if it leads to other national institutions developing their own e-learning capacity, and if it ultimately leads to a gradual expansion of access to Internet technology for the population as a whole.

Facilitate private-sector and international e-learning

An alternative strategy would be to encourage the development of private-sector, non-governmental or international e-learning initiatives from outside the country. The nature of the Internet allows these initiatives to be delivered globally. Furthermore, many of these initiatives are focused on those already in the workforce. This target group has greater disposable income and may also obtain financial support from its employers, thus enabling the full costs of such programmes to be fully funded by the clients. Government support for such initiatives may help better prepare the national workforce and thus support economic development.

The African Virtual University uses satellite TV, videoconferencing and the Internet to give the countries of sub-Saharan Africa direct access to high-quality academic faculty and learning resources from within Africa and other parts of the world (http://www.worldbank.org/knowledgebank/facts/avu.html). Professors from universities around the globe deliver classes in a studio classroom. The course is then beamed by satellite to AVU's learning centres all across Africa, each of which is equipped with an inexpensive satellite dish to receive the signal. During the class, students have an opportunity for real-time interaction with the instructor using phone lines or e-mail. At each participating AVU learning centre, on-site moderators guide the students through the materials and act as liaison with course instructors. All learning centres are equipped with Internet access and at least 50 computers.

Between the launch of its pilot phase in 1997 and 2001, AVU had provided students and professionals in 15 African countries with more than 2,500 hours of interactive instruction in English and French. More than 12,000 students had completed semester-long courses in engineering and the sciences, and more than 2,500 professionals had attended executive and professional management seminars on such topics as Y2K, E-commerce, Entrepreneurship, and Strategy and Innovation. AVU also provides students with access to an on-line digital library with more than 1,000 full-text journals. More than 10,000 students and faculty have opened free e-mail accounts on the AVU Web site.

AVU has established itself as an independent, non-profit organization headquartered in Nairobi, Kenya. Between 2001 and 2003, it will expand to more countries in Africa and reach undergraduate students, faculty, and professionals through three main avenues: learning centres in universities, private franchises, and professional learning centres housed in corporations and non-governmental organizations.

As well as NGOs, a number of private, for-profit organizations are trying to bridge the gap between centralized distribution (such as foreign Web courses or satellite TV) and local support in developing countries. For instance, TeltecGlobal (www.teltecglobal.com) is a 'business services aggregator' offering corporations and governments "a one-stop, turn-key solution for access to 21st century technology, services and education". The TeltecGlobal 'Centre of Influence' is a 'last mile' strategy that provides 'customers' with products and Web-enabled services available through membership in their Community and Business Centres located in developing countries.

TeltecGlobal Community Centres work in conjunction with multinational corporate sponsors, designing an offering of products and services "to meet both community needs and corporate objectives".

Business Centres license operations to local entrepreneurs and 'global government-backed entities' in emerging markets. As with the Community Centres, TeltecGlobal works with the licensees to tailor the products and services to market needs and licensees' goals. TeltecGlobal is a good example of the increasing synergy between technology, education and business.

Governments can facilitate such developments in several ways. They can recognize accreditation from such organizations within their own country. They can encourage partnerships between such international organizations and local universities, colleges and schools. They can provide tax breaks to international e-learning organizations that support national education and training goals, or to students who take such programmes. They can help by providing access to equipment through local learning centres for such initiatives.

However, there are also dangers and disadvantages in depending too heavily on the private sector and international initiatives. The main danger is that inequalities in access to education and training opportunities will increase. Only those who can afford to pay or who have local access to the technology will benefit.

Secondly, the private sector and international universities offering e-learning tend to focus on the profit-generating areas of the curriculum, such as business and information technology programmes. This then leaves government to pick up the costs of other areas, especially those that are specific to a particular nation or culture, or those subject areas that are costly to deliver, such as health sciences.

The third is the impact on national culture. Usually international universities develop the programmes initially for their own students, then look around for a market outside. Most of the programmes from private-sector companies also reflect the language and culture of origin. Such programmes may need considerable adaptation to local languages, culture and history. What is more, what works in a business environment in Australia may be inappropriate in Viet Nam. Such initiatives do nothing to help those who do not speak English or the other predominant international languages used to deliver foreign on-line courses.

Furthermore, relying entirely on international programming does not help a country to develop its own capacity for on-line learning. Everything is imported and over time this could lead to a serious drain on national currencies, as more and more students purchase programmes from other countries.

Lastly, probably the main danger of relying on foreign provision of e-learning is the threat to quality and professional standards. Usually such operations require payment of fees in advance, before enrolment is allowed. The ordinary member of the public will find it very difficult to judge whether a grand-sounding university from another country is a genuine high-quality provider of post-secondary education, or a fly-by-night venture operated out of someone's garage. Even reputable and nationally recognized conventional universities or colleges in other countries may have little experience in on-line learning, or may be running an arms-length 'for-profit' operation that does not make use of the regular faculty.

To combat the danger of poor quality off-shore providers, the Commonwealth of Learning has partnered with a Canadian company, FutureEd, to create quality guidelines for on-line education and training (http://www.futured.com/form/). This is basically a consumer's guide:

> "to give students, parents, and workers the questions they should ask before signing up for an on-line course. Producers of on-line learning – public universities, colleges and school boards, not-for-profits, commercial firms – can then use the guide to meet consumer expectations."
> (Commonwealth of Learning, March 2001: http://www.col.org/newsrelease/0103qualityguide.htm).

Nevertheless, some governments may feel that they too have a responsibility both to protect their own institutions from external and possibly unfair competition, and to protect the public from exploitation from foreign operations. In such circumstances, they may wish to try and regulate the accreditation of foreign e-learning initiatives, an issue that has been discussed in the previous chapter.

Using e-learning to transform post-secondary education

Many governments are concerned with the need for the reform of their post-secondary institutions. In many countries, demand for college and university places far exceeds the supply. High quality and effective post-secondary education is available only to the rich. Often the more wealthy leave their country for education overseas, and many fail to return, thus depriving a country of those most able to transform the country, and draining the country of national currency and future tax revenues. In many countries, professors in the public colleges and universities are poorly paid and overworked, often taking several parallel jobs, and therefore have little time for research or adequate preparation for teaching. As a result, students are often poorly taught in very large lecture classes in the public sector. Governments meanwhile struggle to repay debt, the middle classes resent taxes, and hence governments have inadequate resources to invest adequately in public post-secondary education.

It is not surprising then that **governments in a number of countries are looking at e-learning as one possible means for making post-secondary education more cost-effective, more learner-centred and more economically relevant.** This tendency is just as prevalent incidentally in the more economically advanced countries as in poorer countries, as the Western Governors' University has demonstrated.

The cost-effectiveness argument will be examined more closely in the next chapter. Here the emphasis will be on transforming the culture of post-secondary institutions, to make them more learner-centred and more economically relevant.

There is no doubt that involving professors and instructors in e-learning can help revitalize teaching and learning in an institution. For younger professors, especially those with prior experience in using computer technology at school or home, teaching with technology is 'cool'. It also helps connect them with the students, who themselves see the use of computers as fun and 'cool'. For more experienced and senior professors, e-learning can be a welcome change from oversized lecture classes and doing the same thing over many years.

However, for the revitalization of an institution through the use of e-learning to happen on a wide scale, there have to be some powerful incentives. Research on successful innovative practices (see, for instance, Rogers, 1995) has indicated that there is a normal curve for the adoption of an innovative practice (see *Figure 2*).

At one end of the curve is a small percentage of early adopters, enthusiasts who are committed to the use of, in this case, e-learning (group a). In some respects, little needs to be done to encourage these early adopters. They are committed to change and to doing whatever they can to make the innovation work. They will often work against all odds, and even active discouragement from colleagues and the institutional management. However, they usually constitute a small percentage of the total workforce (between 10-15 per cent is typical). For this reason, while they can be very important catalysts for change, without further action from management, the impact of early adopters on the way the institution operates is relatively small. They are often used by management as a token of an institution's innovative practice, but in reality the rest of the institution is unchanged.

Figure 2.   The curve of adoption for innovation

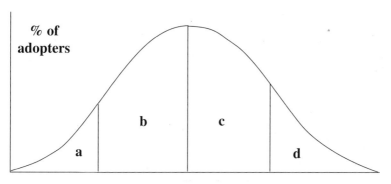

Resistance to adoption

73

The next group (b) is the most important for targeting innovative practice. These group members have not yet adopted a new practice, but are open to change. They also constitute a sizeable proportion of staff (around 30-40 per cent). In universities and colleges, they are often making a rational decision not to adopt e-learning. They may see its advantages, but because the necessary institutional rewards and support infrastructures are not in place, they are not willing to change. In a university, e-learning may be seen as a time-consuming distraction from research. An institution's management can change this core group of mainstream teachers by putting in appropriate reward systems for adopting e-learning and the necessary supporting infrastructure, such as technical help and easy access to the technology. Management can also help these group members to see the clear benefits both to themselves and their students from the adoption of e-learning.

The third group (c) members are more hostile to change. They are not likely to be influenced so easily by management actions. However, they are more likely to be influenced by other mainstream colleagues who do change (the 'b's), and who do demonstrate benefits and advantages of change. Thus if they see their respected mainstream colleagues embracing e-learning, and can see that their colleagues and the students are clearly benefiting from this, they themselves may slowly embrace the change.

The last group (d) members are strongly hostile to change. They may have deep ideological or philosophical objections to the change, or may see their status or position challenged by the change. They are unlikely ever to embrace the innovation. Fortunately, though, they tend to be a relatively small minority of the workforce.

It is clear from experience that this theory of change is particularly relevant to the adoption of e-learning. The point is made to show that it is not an easy process, and requires investment in resources, a carefully focused management strategy, and an understanding of the need for a change to the culture of the organization. There must be clearly defined and observable benefits for both instructors and students as a result of the change. It will take time – several years – before the full impact of the change becomes evident.

Governments then looking at e-learning as a means to bring about change in their institutions must ask themselves the following questions:

(a) Do the institutions have the necessary resources (financial, technical and management) to support e-learning? If they do not, change will remain locked within the early adopter community and the core of the institution will remain unchanged.

(b) What can government do to facilitate the process of change towards greater use of e-learning? It is much easier for instance to create a new organization and recruit those committed to change, than to change institutions from within. On the other hand, creating a new institution will not address the systemic problems within the existing institutions.

(c) Is e-learning the most appropriate means to bring about change; would the same investment in resources and effort in other areas bring better results?

The second issue is even more challenging, and that is whether the adoption of e-learning will result in a more learner-centred approach to education and training. The goal of learner-centred teaching is to help students to take responsibility for their own learning, so that they can become independent lifelong learners, a critical skill in a knowledge-based economy and society. This is not necessarily a technological issue, but can be done perhaps even more easily within a face-to-face classroom context.

However, one reason why on-line learning has become popular in some institutions is because it does allow for asynchronous, time-independent communication between learners, and between learners and the instructor. Thus it increases flexibility for the students (and instructors).

Furthermore, and perhaps more importantly, electronic administrative systems, such as Web registration, electronic fee payments, and Web portals, through which an individual student can access all the information relevant to that student's study, are much more student friendly than campus-based administrative systems based on office hours, queuing in line, and dealing with busy and not always helpful administrative staff.

Thus there is without doubt potential for making an institution's teaching and administration more learner-centred through the adoption of e-learning. However, this too depends on major changes in working practice by both teachers and administrators, heavy investment in new technologies and training, and could also be achieved by methods other than e-learning.

Lastly, to what extent will the introduction of e-learning lead to a better-trained workforce? Certainly, there are advantages to the adoption of e-learning for company training, where the company has a dispersed workforce and access to the technology for business purposes.

In the public sector, however, the value of e-learning with respect to workforce development will depend on the main areas of employment within a particular country. In countries heavily dependent on resource extraction, agriculture, and heavy manufacturing, there is likely to be a much smaller market for those with skills developed through e-learning compared with more traditional methods. In countries moving towards more knowledge-based industries or already heavily dependent on them, e-learning will be much more relevant. (This issue will be discussed further in the last chapter.)

Thus it is unlikely that the adoption of e-learning to bring about fundamental changes within a country's higher education system will be sufficient on its own. It will depend on the particular business and industrial context of a country, and above all on the availability of the necessary resources to ensure the successful implementation of e-learning. It is not a cheap option, and there may be better alternatives to bring about a revitalization of existing institutions.

Developing an e-learning business sector

Countries with more advanced economies are looking to build a large, national e-learning business sector that can create jobs and bring in revenues from other countries. Governments such as Canada are developing Web-based national directories of e-learning programmes and providers, and looking at ways to stimulate a Canadian e-learning business sector. In Australia, the federal Department of Education, Training and Youth Affairs has been active in facilitating and promoting Australian e-learning providers in their international efforts.

2) *Developing a national archive of e-learning materials*

Another development is the creation of national or international archives of on-line learning materials. These can range from whole curricula on-line, such as the programmes or courses of an institution, to very small objects, such as a graphic or animation, that can be accessed over the Web and downloaded for use in a particular piece of teaching.

A good example of this approach is Brazil's Biblioteca Virtual (Virtual Library) developed as part of the Escola do Futoro project at the Universidade de São Paulo. This provides an archive of works in Portuguese that can be used in the Brazilian school or university systems (see http://www.bibvirt.futuro.usp.br/).

Some institutions are now putting their whole curricula up on to the Web. Massachusetts Institute of Technology has made its curriculum available free of charge through the OpenCourseWare project (http://Web.mit.edu/oki/). The idea behind MIT OpenCourseWare (MIT OCW) is to make MIT course materials that are used in the teaching of almost all undergraduate and graduate subjects available on the Web, free of charge, to any user anywhere in the world. As their Web site says:

> "MIT OpenCourseWare will provide the content of, but is not a substitute for, an MIT education. The most fundamental cornerstone of the learning process at MIT is the interaction between faculty and students in the classroom, and amongst students themselves on campus... Depending on the particular class or the style in which the course is taught, the site could include material such as lecture notes, course outlines, reading lists, and assignments for each course. More technically

sophisticated content will be encouraged. The materials on the OCW site will be open and freely available worldwide for non-commercial purposes such as research and education, providing an extraordinary resource, free of charge, which others can adapt to their own needs. Faculty at colleges and universities around the world can use the OCW materials to develop new curricula and specific courses. These materials might be of particular value in developing countries that are trying to expand their higher education systems rapidly. Individual learners could draw upon the materials for self-study or supplementary use."

At a more detailed level, databases and repositories for print, audio, graphics, video and multimedia are being made accessible to other users either free or commercially. One common term for such materials is 'learning objects', and there are various attempts to develop common international standards that will facilitate quick and easy search, access, and, where necessary, financial transactions for the use of such materials.

Any government interested in establishing a database of locally developed on-line materials will need to ensure that it is aware of the growth of international standards in these areas (see Porter, 2001, for an excellent discussion of this issue). It will also need to be aware of the issues around copyright and intellectual property (see Bates, 2000, for a more detailed discussion of this issue).

It is important to recognize though that education is as much about process as it is about product. As MIT carefully explains, education is about the interaction between students and teachers, as well as access to knowledge. Nevertheless, the development of free or low-cost learning materials on-line can be extremely valuable to any teacher anywhere in the world, and can lead to huge savings in time and expense in developing materials from scratch.

3) *Do nothing*

This is always an option for government. **Some governments**, after a careful analysis of the advantages and disadvantages of e-learning within the specific context of their own nation, **may legitimately conclude that e-learning is not appropriate, affordable, or a priority at this time.**

The danger of course is to assume without analysis that e-learning is not appropriate. **Even if a country has no intention of investing or supporting e-learning internally, it would be dangerous to ignore the fact that e-learning from other sources is becoming rapidly available, especially to the wealthy or technological elite within a country.** This issue will be discussed more fully in the final chapter.

Conclusion

Three more radical strategies than building on the existing post-secondary system have been considered: creating a new national e-university; supporting private-sector, non-governmental, and off-shore institutions' efforts in e-learning; and using e-learning to revitalize and transform post-secondary educational institutions.

In addition three other strategies – building an e-learning business sector, developing a national archive of e-learning materials, and doing nothing – were also briefly discussed.

There are clear advantages in creating a new e-learning institution from scratch, either nationally or, even more so, regionally. The main challenge will be adequately funding such an institution, and if developed on a regional basis, securing collaboration and support from several other countries.

There are plenty of private sector and external providers of e-learning services already, and this will grow rapidly over the next few years. There are some clear short-term benefits of government working to facilitate and support the e-learning initiatives of such providers, especially for the lifelong learning market and workforce development. However, this is not likely to be a sufficient strategy on its own. **Over the long run, dependency on private sector or international agencies for e-learning will have serious implications for equity**

of access to educational services, the development of a national e-learning capacity, and national and cultural identity.

The hope that e-learning will help foster institutional renewal and revitalize the teaching in post-secondary institutions is an even more contentious issue. It might, but it would need a substantial and sustainable effort in other areas as well, such as rewards for innovation, a skilled management committed to fostering change, adequate resources to support e-learning, and a teaching profession open to new ideas. There may be more practical ways to revitalize education at the tertiary level, and e-learning will not avoid the need for more investment in the system.

The creation of a national e-learning business sector is also a stiff challenge. There are two or three successful on-line courseware companies in the world (e.g. WebCT and Blackboard), all now American owned. The development of multimedia learning materials requires a highly skilled workforce and substantial financial investment. It is a high-risk industry – as much a high risk as the dot.com companies, of which it is in fact a sub-sector. Nevertheless there may be opportunities in certain language and cultural sectors with high demand and large populations (e.g. China, Latin America, the Indian sub-continent).

Governments can and should play a major role in creating local, national and indigenous learning materials, and making them available through some form of national or regional archive. The Brazilian Virtual Biblioteca is a good example of what can be done for relatively little investment. This however requires government to ensure that on-line materials developed by publicly supported post-secondary institutions are cleared for copyright for national use, and co-ordination between institutions creating the materials so that they are easily available through a common Web site and using common technical standards.

Lastly, governments can always do nothing. There may be a case for this where the national telecommunications and Internet infrastructure is so bad that access is limited to all but the very rich and powerful, and the government is satisfied that the impact of foreign providers will be small or insignificant for national culture or identity. In all other cases, governments need to examine carefully the implications for national development of e-learning, even if the internal capacity for developing e-learning is quite small.

V. The costs and benefits of e-learning

General guidelines on the costs of e-learning

The cost structures of e-learning are different from those of face-to-face teaching and from distance education based on the mass-media technologies of broadcasting, video, audio and print.

There has in fact been very little research done on the costs of e-learning. Also, costs cannot be looked at in isolation. It is always possible to do things more cheaply if one is prepared to sacrifice quality. Benefits or cost-effectiveness must also be considered. This is a critical point because as with face-to-face teaching, e-learning can vary considerably in how it is designed, developed and delivered, and these variations in methods will affect the costs and the effectiveness of e-learning.

However, from what research has been done, and from experience to date of developing and delivering e-learning programmes, some guidelines on the costs of e-learning can be given:

1. **E-learning is not a cheap alternative to face-to-face teaching.** Its main benefit is to improve the quality of instruction, rather than reduce costs.

2. **The average cost per student of e-learning will in general be greater than the average cost per student of traditional distance education based on a mix of broadcasting and print.** However, for courses enrolling less than 100 students per course offering, the cost differences per student between e-learning and traditional distance education are slight.

3. The direct costs of e-learning will be roughly similar to face-to-face teaching for courses enrolling between 20 to 30 students per course offering, over a five-year period.

4. For courses with less than 20 enrolments per offering, the direct costs of face-to-face teaching are likely to be lower than for e-

learning. For courses with more than 30 enrolments per offering, the direct costs of e-learning per student are likely to be slightly lower, provided that similar teacher/student ratios are maintained for both methods as numbers change.

5. If there is large demand for a course, and *if teacher/student ratios are maintained by hiring more instructors*, e-learning becomes progressively cheaper than face-to-face teaching as numbers increase. However, **it is not always possible to reach the enrolments needed in e-learning to reach the break-even point over face-to-face teaching**, without some major restructuring of the teaching within a department or institution. Both forms of teaching become progressively cheaper per student if class sizes are increased without maintaining the same teacher/student ratio, but quality of interaction with students will drop.

6. Face-to-face teaching in post-secondary education has very high indirect/overhead costs (buildings, etc.); the indirect/overhead costs of e-learning have not been well researched, but appear to be substantially lower.

7. Some of the benefits of e-learning are the same as those for face-to-face teaching, such as interaction between students, and interaction with the instructor; other benefits are different, such as increased student flexibility with e-learning, and access instantly to global resources. Other benefits depend on circumstances; for instance, for some working adults e-learning can increase access, but may limit access for students going on to university from high school.

8. Excluding the cost of tuition, with e-learning there can be a transfer of some costs from the institution to full-time students, but this will depend on circumstances. **For part-time or working adults who *already have a computer and Internet* access, e-learning could result in considerable cost-savings, such as traveling and lost work time.**

9. In assessing the costs and benefits of e-learning, it is essential to consider the type of student at whom e-learning is aimed. **The**

benefits of e-learning are much clearer for working adults and more mature students. There are also benefits for younger full-time students if e-learning is combined with face-to-face teaching (mixed mode), although costs are likely to be higher.

10. Few institutions within the university and college sector are making large profits so far from e-learning. Some are breaking even, and a few are making a small return (up to 15 per cent) on investment. The market for cost-recovery or profit-making however is limited to certain areas such as continuing professional education, business programmes, and programmes on information technology. It is also a very competitive market, with many new suppliers of programming.

11. Much more research needs to be done on the costs and benefits of e-learning *and* on different forms of face-to-face teaching. In particular, there needs to be a focus on the costs of mixed-mode teaching, on the cost of different methods of developing e-learning, and on the comparative indirect/overhead costs for face-to-face teaching and e-learning. There is an important role to be played by government here, in funding and supporting such research.

12. Accounting systems in most universities and colleges are not set up to provide the necessary information to compare the costs of different forms of teaching. Governments could encourage institutions to move to an activity-based system of costing, which would enable such comparisons to be made more easily.

These guidelines should be treated with some caution, because of the lack of extensive research on costs and benefits of both e-learning and different forms of face-to-face teaching at a post-secondary level.

The above conclusions are nevertheless based on results from previous research and from the experience of organizations running university and college on-line courses. This research, and the methodology on which it is based, are summarized in Appendix 1. Those wishing to understand more fully the cost structures of e-learning are strongly recommended to consult Appendix 1.

The above conclusions are also influenced by the work of the Distance Education and Technology unit (DE&T) at the University of British Columbia. This unit has been tracking the costs of its on-line distance education delivery since it started developing on-line courses in 1996. In 2001 it was offering approximately 60 Web-based on-line courses, as well as 40 print-based courses developed before 1996.

These guidelines, and factors influencing these guidelines, will be looked at in a little more detail below.

Factors influencing the costs of e-learning

The costs (and benefits) of e-learning are influenced by several factors: the method of developing and delivering e-learning; the amount of multimedia within the course; teacher/student ratios; the status and salary of instructors; number of students per course offering; and the number of course offerings before the course is withdrawn.

Developing and delivering e-learning

There is a wide variety of methods being used to develop and deliver e-learning programmes. The most prevalent has been what has been described (Bates, 2000) as the Lone Ranger approach (after an old Hollywood cowboy film and television series). In this approach, individual professors or instructors work on their own, sometimes helped by a small grant that supports a graduate student. They work in isolation from their colleagues, and get very little help or support from the administration for their efforts.

This method has attracted strong criticism (Bates, 2000). Essentially it is very time-consuming for the professor, who is often untrained in instructional or graphic design skills. A great deal of time is spent in learning how to use the technology, and the results are often of poor quality and idiosyncratic. Thus the material developed cannot be used by or shared with other professors, who are often working in a similar isolated way. As Karelis (1999) points out, this prevents the much vaunted economies of scale of technology use from being achieved. The use of technology remains a cottage industry.

More importantly, the use of technology adds cost to the system, without any great improvement in learning benefits.

An alternative model, used in professional distance education units as well as commercial media production, is the project management method. A project is created with the following features:

- a cash budget;
- members of a team with different skills, ranging from subject expert to instructional designer to Web programmer;
- an allocation of set time in days for each member of the team to work on the project;
- a schedule;
- a deadline;
- a product at the end (e.g. a course, or unit of teaching, or a CD-ROM).

The team has to work within the time and budget constraints.

The up-front costs of a project management approach may appear to be more costly than those of an individual professor working alone. However, **project teams using off-the-shelf course development tools** such as WebCT or Blackboard **can cut down dramatically on the amount of time needed by the professor to develop materials,** once the team has agreed a template and framework for the course design. This is true not only for the development of the course, but also for the delivery, using course design tools such as frequently asked questions, standard on-line test software, group assignments and group discussions. With a project management approach, the end result is also usually of much higher quality.

With face-to-face teaching, costs tend to increase with student numbers, if the teacher/student ratio is held constant. If it is not, class size increases, and interaction between student and teacher is reduced per student. Lastly, face-to-face teaching costs are more or less the same from year to year, in that work done the previous year must be repeated again the following year. Thus if teacher/student ratios are maintained, the overall cost of face-to-face teaching varies more or less in proportion to the number of students.

In traditional print-based distance education, with or without a strong television or audio component, development and delivery are usually totally separated. Development is done once, with very minor maintenance of the course from year to year. The same materials are used from year to year. Delivery (the tutoring, which is mainly the marking of written assignments) is often done by contract instructors. Thus a print-based distance education course, especially with broadcasting components, has high development costs that are fixed, i.e. independent of the number of students who eventually take the course. It will however have relatively low delivery costs (cost of print and audio/video materials, which students often pay for, plus the cost of marking assignments). Delivery costs are dependent on the number of students, and hence increase with students, but at a lesser rate than for face-to-face teaching, as much of the 'work' is contained within the materials (readings, activities, etc.). Thus teacher/student ratios can be increased.

On-line courses have fixed development costs. Web-based courses are usually slightly cheaper to develop initially than print-based distance courses, because of the use of course authoring tools, and the transfer of existing materials such as slides to the Web. However, web-based courses tend to have higher maintenance costs than a print-based course, as changes can easily be made with a Web course from year to year. (DE&T allows approximately 25 per cent of the first year development costs for maintenance of a Web course each year, which means that over four years the course can be completely renewed.) Print-based courses however may need major revisions or total redesign after several years, and it is easy to build up a large maintenance 'debt'.

Media costs

Broadcasting, especially television, requires heavy up-front costs that can be justified only with very large numbers of student enrolments (usually over 1,000 per course offering). The same applies to Web-based courses that require a lot of multimedia production. Media production costs can vary from $10,000 to $250,000 for a CD-ROM, for instance, and can be justified again only by very large numbers of course enrolments, or by the separate sale of the materials.

Teacher/student ratio and the status of instructors

Another factor that dramatically influences the costs of e-learning, traditional print-based distance education, and face-to-face teaching, is the teacher/student ratio, and, just as importantly, the status of the instructor.

Much of the expansion of conventional university education has resulted in a gradual increase in class size, the use of adjunct, lower paid part-time instructors and teaching assistants, or a combination of all these. The result of this has been reduced exposure of students to the tenured research professors.

If class sizes increase, then individual teacher/student interaction decreases. Increasing class sizes also means a move towards more transmissive instructional methods, such as lecturing, and away from more critical discussion of issues. One also has to assume that the increased use of less experienced adjunct professors and teaching assistants must lead to a lower quality of interaction than if students were taught by full research professors. Thus while average costs may drop as class size increases, there is a significant shift also in quality.

A big difference between print-based distance education and on-line learning is the interaction between students, and between students and instructor. While an instructor may be limited only by the time required to mark assignments in a traditional print-based distance education course, an on-line instructor has to organize and participate in the on-line discussion forums, as well as mark assignments. In short this means that on-line instructors can handle fewer students per course offering than a print-based distance education tutor. Thus there are lower economies of scale for on-line teaching than for traditional print-based teaching.

However, also with Web courses much of the transmission of information is through the materials rather than the professor. Thus while instructors may spend more time interacting with students than on a print and/or broadcast-based course, it is still less than in teaching a face-to-face class of equivalent size. Thus **an important qualitative**

benefit is that Web courses combine access to a wide range of knowledge and information with discussion and dialogue.

Lastly, in both print/broadcast-based distance education and Web-based courses, adjunct part-time instructors can be used to supplement the main subject expert or research professor in the delivery of the course. They work to the materials designed by the research professor, but concentrate on marking, and in on-line courses, on moderating group discussions.

The use of lower paid adjunct instructors or tutors helps reduce the delivery costs. Adjunct, part-time instructors of course are also often used in face-to-face teaching, but in both forms of distance teaching, the research professor can more easily supervise the work of the adjunct instructor. Also, in many institutions using e-learning, the research professor or subject expert who designed an on-line course also usually tutors the course, for at least the first year. Thus the savings on lower paid adjunct professors is less than with the print-based courses.

Quality, of course, can always be sacrificed to save money. Web-based courses can be designed so that there is little on-line discussion or interaction with the instructor. However, this would result in one of the main qualitative advantages of e-learning being lost. This is an important point, because some of the plans for e-learning suggest that e-learning is primarily the delivery of unmoderated materials over the Web. Consequently the importance of interaction between students and teacher is underestimated, and hence there is insufficient allowance for the high ongoing cost of delivery.

Student numbers

Another critical factor is the combination of the number of students per course offering, and the number of times a course is offered. Because there are fixed costs in the development of on-line and print-based courses, a high proportion of costs fall in the first year of development. With face-to-face teaching there is less variation in costs from year to year. Thus in making comparisons, costs need to be averaged over the life of a course, to take account of student numbers over the whole course.

Level of activity

Another factor is the level of activity. There are major start-up costs for a department in moving to on-line learning for the first time. Some costs, such as for setting up administrative systems such as on-line registration and fee payment, instructional design, and server maintenance, need to be spread over a large number of courses to be viable. Outsourcing to an e-learning company might be an alternative, at a higher cost, for a smaller number of courses.

Centralizing activities may not be popular in a decentralized institution, such as a research university. However, a central unit that supports e-learning development, delivery, student support and, above all, on-line student administration, usually brings an increase both in quality and in cost savings (see Bartolic and Bates, 1999, for a full discussion of this).

Mixed mode

The costs of mixed-mode teaching are even more complex, combining as they do a reduced face-to-face teaching component with on-line learning. More study needs to be done on the costs and the effectiveness of this model.

Therefore in making any comparisons of costs between face-to-face teaching, mixed-mode teaching, traditional print-based/broadcast distance education, and e-learning, one has to take into account teacher/student ratios, qualifications and experience of the instructors, and the method of working (lectures, seminars, project management, mixed mode, distance education, etc.).

Implications of the cost studies for national learning strategies

Good quality e-learning that exploits the interactive and design characteristics of Web-based learning is not a cheap alternative to face-to-face teaching. While e-learning allows for some economies of scale compared to face-to-face teaching, they are not as great as those provided by more traditional print-based and mass-media models of distance education.

For e-learning to be economically justified, institutions will need to act strategically and restructure their activities, implementing project management and widening access to out-of-state or international students. In doing so, they will enter a highly competitive environment.

One of the main benefits of e-learning comes from increasing interaction in on-line discussion forums, thus facilitating critical thinking and active learning. Thus e-learning, rather than reducing costs, helps to increase the quality of learning, at least over traditional distance education, and also possibly over large face-to-face lectures. However, to achieve an improvement in quality, there must be investment in design and development, and a good teacher/student ratio for delivery, although some of the tutors need not be full research professors.

One of the possible benefits of e-learning is that it may be a way of adding students at lower marginal costs to an expanding system if the overheads of traditional campuses are taken into account. In many institutions, the direct costs of teaching are only half the total costs needed to support the teaching. The rest comes from building, grounds maintenance, etc. There will also be indirect costs such as the technology infrastructure associated with e-learning, and these can be substantial, but **once the networks are in place, the marginal cost of expanding student numbers through e-learning may be much lower than building new campuses or campus buildings.** However, this could be determined only by doing a careful cost-benefit analysis within a particular context.

There is a tendency to think that e-learning could be a big money earner, allowing publicly funded institutions to cross-subsidize some of their activities, or to allow private-sector companies to come in and take some of the pressure off government to provide education and training.

First of all, what little studies have been done suggest that the true cost of offering the equivalent of a one-year full-time Master's programme on-line is around $12,000 per student in North America. In jurisdictions where 80 per cent or more of the cost of post-secondary education is subsidized by government, most people are just not going to be able to afford the full cost of e-learning. Asking students to pay the full price of e-learning programmes will inflate greatly the costs of higher education for those students.

However, **there are likely to be niche markets in continuing professional education, business, biotechnology and information technology where students or their employers will be willing to pay the full cost for an e-learning programme. Although it will not be much cheaper than the full cost of campus-based education, it will probably be more convenient.**

Only in the most developed countries, and only in those institutions where students come from mainly middle-class families, are students likely to have access to computers at home. **In most countries, institutions wanting to provide e-learning for traditional undergraduate students will have to provide the equipment for such students. There will be a high cost in doing this**, given the rapid obsolescence of computer equipment.

However, there will be an increasing market of those students already in the workforce who will either have the necessary disposable income to buy a computer and pay for Internet access from home, or who will have access at work through their employers. **On balance, most mature students will almost certainly prefer e-learning courses to courses where they have to travel to a campus at fixed times.**

These students are most likely to be served by the private sector. Nevertheless, there will also be opportunities for public-sector institutions with strong research areas, or strong in-house e-learning or distance education units, to provide continuing professional education for those already in the workforce, on a cost-recoverable or profit-generating basis. However, this will depend on the infrastructure being in place within the public institution, and the interest and the willingness of professors to develop such courses. This will require the money generated to be returned to the department and even the individual professors.

Cost issues

In some ways, there is little government can do directly to deal with the cost issues of e-learning, other than support the national technology infrastructure, and provide education and training to institutions on the issues of the costs and benefits of e-learning.

It is very important that government, institutions, and professors interested in e-learning understand the structure of costs in e-learning, face-to-face teaching and traditional distance education, and the relation to benefits.

Government could fund research into costs and benefits and help disseminate the results to the institutions. Most of all, governments could look carefully at activity-based costing, and test whether this could be applied to their institutions, so that institutions can more effectively assess the costs and benefits of e-learning.

VI. Funding strategies

The importance of funding as a government strategy for e-learning

Funding is probably the most powerful lever that government has in influencing the development of post-secondary education and training. This does not mean that spending need increase to unmanageable proportions in order to foster and sustain e-learning. It will be seen that there is much that governments and institutions can do within their existing funding to support e-learning.

Nevertheless, e-learning is not an option that comes without additional costs. There are both the costs of investment, to kick-start e-learning activities, and the costs of sustaining them. How can institutions find resources to fund e-learning at a time when universities and colleges are under increasing pressure to reduce costs, and when government fiscal policy is often to reduce rather than increase public spending? This is perhaps the most difficult of all the issues surrounding the development of e-learning.

There are several funding strategies to be considered:

- reallocate existing resources (both at a government and institutional level);
- create a new e-learning institution;
- increase student tuition fees;
- target short-term grants for e-learning projects;
- increase government baseline funding for institutions;
- use e-learning to absorb extra enrolments;
- encourage cost-recoverable e-learning programmes;
- allow public-sector institutions to establish for-profit companies.

This chapter looks at the advantages and disadvantages of each of these strategies.

The need to fund e-learning developments in a sustainable manner

A study by the American Productivity & Quality Centre (1999) found that teaching staff are often not adequately trained in the use of the technology for on-line learning. They also are often unaware of the importance of project management, or of the instructional design and media production skills required for the development of high quality on-line courses. More importantly, teaching is often poorly done after the Web site is designed, in terms of managing on-line discussions and assignments, and students are often inadequately supported or instructors are overwhelmed with student communications.

Institutions often do not provide teaching staff with sufficient technical, media production or instructional design support or training in on-line learning, and as a result instructors often complain of the extra workload that results. **Many** of these **problems are due to inadequate funding or financial strategies for e-learning, resulting in programmes being unsustainable or under-resourced and hence of poor quality.**

Many institutions (and governments) have assumed that the introduction of e-learning is a zero-based funding issue: there are no extra costs. This is an incorrect assumption. It has been shown in the previous chapter that e-learning is not a cheap option to face-to-face teaching. It has to be approached in the same way as any other new line of business: it needs investment. Businesses invest in new technology not necessarily to save money, but to obtain competitive advantage. The main advantage for public institutions and governments investing in e-learning is not likely to be to save money, but to improve the quality of learning, and to develop workforce skills that will eventually facilitate economic development. **Governments and institutions that think that e-learning can be successfully introduced without additional investment should not go this route.**

Reallocation

The reallocation of existing funding is probably the most realistic option for supporting e-learning. This of course means that difficult choices have to be made. Something has to be given up or replaced by e-learning. Thus policy decisions have to be made about the importance of e-learning relative to other educational, social or economic issues at a government level, and about methods of teaching and learning at an institutional level. This is the acid test of the perceived value of e-learning.

If e-learning is to be a sustainable activity, eventually it will need to be funded from regular operating budgets. If e-learning is considered important for national development or for improving the quality of teaching within institutions, it needs to become a core part of the activity of post-secondary institutions. Similarly, governments may have to re-allocate funds to enable initial investments to be made, and to cover the legitimate additional costs to institutions of incorporating e-learning into their regular activities.

In the end, reallocation may require difficult decisions if resources are to be made available for e-learning. This may require weak or uneconomic teaching departments to be closed, savings made in other budgets such as buildings and equipment, or funding for other government programmes to be reduced, in order to free up the money needed for e-learning. The biggest problem with reallocation as a strategy is that in their self-interest, teaching staff will inevitably strongly oppose any moves to cut academic positions or departments in order to fund the use of e-learning.

This is not to argue that e-learning *should* replace other activities. Governments and institutions, as will be seen in the final chapter, may make the decision that e-learning is not the highest priority or the most desirable direction to go. However, once e-learning does become a desired strategy, then for it to be sustained, painful choices will need to be made.

Probably the most practical reallocation option for an institution is to replace some face-to-face activities with e-learning, and to make more effective use of teaching staff through the use of the technology. For instance, by using Web-based materials, on-line group discussions and e-mail, classroom activities may be reduced by one or two sessions a week, freeing up the instructors for work on e-learning activities.

Core teaching materials may be created that can be adapted for a variety of different courses or programmes, thus reducing the amount of time instructors need to deliver new programmes. Materials that are developed for on-campus students can be modified and adapted for cost-recoverable continuing professional education programmes, thus generating more revenues for a department.

The message for government is that before any additional funds are allocated to institutions for e-learning activities, institutions should be able to indicate how they will use such funds efficiently. One way to do this would be by requiring institutions to develop a teaching and technology plan that indicates how e-learning will become a sustainable operation within the institution's regular budget.

Another prime target for reallocation at both a government and institutional level is through an analysis of the balance of funding between infrastructure, administrative applications, and educational applications of technology. Investment in technology infrastructure and administrative information technology systems tends to precede and largely exceed investment in educational applications. It may be worthwhile for government and institutions to take an audit of relative spending in these three areas. In some institutions, it may be time to slow down investment in further improvements to the technology infrastructure or administrative systems, and reallocate at least some of the resources historically devoted to these other areas into educational applications such as e-learning.

Similarly, government may be giving undue priority to investment in technological infrastructure, and not enough to the resources needed to make use of the infrastructure. Increases in capital expenditure will usually need to be accompanied by increases in operating expenditure, or the capital expenditure will be wasted. This means having a good understanding of the relationship between capital and operating expenditures. For instance, often **for every dollar spent on technology infrastructure, ten dollars are needed to operate and use the infrastructure.** This is certainly true of e-learning. Alternatively, if priorities for classroom teaching have historically dominated budget allocations, it may be time to switch resources into technical support for faculty.

These approaches, however, require a management structure that enables such cross-divisional and often cross-budgetary transfers or changes to be made. For instance, it may be necessary to transfer some funds out of one budget, such as the Ministry of Industry or Communications, into another, such as the Ministry of Education, as priorities between infrastructure investment and educational applications change. Certainly, moving funding out of one budget holder's area into another's will be very difficult, unless there is a fully agreed vision and strategy for e-learning at the highest level.

Create a new e-learning institution

In *Chapter 4* it was pointed out that there are strong reasons for creating a new national e-learning institution, especially in countries where resources are limited. It was also stated however that substantial and continuous funding, in the order of several million dollars a year (or the equivalent in local currencies) would be needed at a minimum.

It is critical that the funding base is realistic and based on an understanding of the costs and benefits of e-learning. For instance, Kim Beazley, the Australian leader of the Labor Party, stated that their proposed e-university would be funded at half the level per student of face-to-face teaching in conventional campuses. This is likely to be a gross underestimate of the true cost of providing e-learning at a quality comparable to conventional university education. The additional funding needed will almost certainly have to be made up by employer subsidies or increased fees paid by students.

There will certainly be more opportunities to maximize the economies of scale of e-learning by creating a new institution rather than adding e-learning to conventional institutions. It may be possible to reduce student unit costs by up to 25 per cent through a large, national institution focused solely on e-learning, particularly if it makes use of infrastructure already provided by other campus-based institutions. However, the reality is that if the cost of providing the necessary technical support to ensure access is included, unit costs per student will not be dramatically below those for face-to-face teaching.

Increase student fees

Some institutions in North America are already passing some of the costs of technology investment directly on to the students by means of a student technology fee. Sonoma State University in California introduced a student technology fee that applied to all students, as well as requiring students to provide their own computer. The fee was used to provide technical help and support for students, to improve the local area network, to provide docking ports for portables, and to make available easy access to public computers in public places on campus. Students themselves play a large role in managing this fund and in approving the level of the fee. Collège Boréal in Ontario, Canada, levied a fee of C$1,200 (US$800) per student per year. For this, each student received a laptop computer on lease, with the option of buying it at a much reduced price after two years, as a result of an agreement with IBM.

There are several reasons why a growing number of institutions are imposing special student technology fees. The first is that the need for students to access computers for study purposes is 'new', and that since there is no existing budget for this, it is necessary to find a way to raise the additional money. Since students also think that the use of computers in their teaching is important, they are likely to agree to this. In other words, it is easier to sell an increase in fees for this specific purpose than a general fee increase.

Another reason is that the institution has not accepted the use of technology for teaching as a core academic activity; it is supplementary and optional. However, students will vote in favour of such a fee (as they did at both Sonoma State and Collège Boréal) only if the benefits to them are clear. In particular, the institution needs to make very clear the added value to students of using computers for learning.

Furthermore, some may question the equity of charging students an additional fee for technology access. This increasingly moves education out of the reach of those from families with low incomes. Also, students in most institutions are not charged for access to the library or for the use of lecture theatres. Why should they be charged extra because they are using often their own computer?

A more justifiable argument could be made for increasing student fees if the e-learning programmes are focused primarily at those in the workforce. They may pay a higher level of fees than students leaving high school, but this of course will depend on people in the workforce having access to the technology and the necessary disposal income to cover the costs.

Targeted *short-term grants* for *e-learning*

Special short-term one- or three-year grants from government to encourage technological innovation for teaching have prompted many universities and colleges to move more vigorously into the use of e-learning. The government of Alberta in Canada for instance created an 'envelope' of funding held back from the general university operating grants to encourage innovation. This was applied for on a grant basis by individual faculty and instructors. Preference was given to proposals that fostered inter-institutional collaboration.

Earmarked government funding is a good strategy to get institutions to pay attention to e-learning, particularly if the money is taken from what they would otherwise have been allocated. However there are also disadvantages or limitations to such a strategy.

The first of course is that this interferes with the autonomy of the institution to make the most appropriate strategic decisions about where to invest resources. Indeed, a strategy such as the government of Alberta's can actually undermine an institution's attempt to manage e-learning cost-effectively. Government is often not in the best position to judge the quality of a particular e-learning application or the resources needed to sustain it. Such grants distract faculty from an institution's own priorities.

Another strategy, particularly popular in institutions in the USA, is to rely on grants from external organizations, such as research councils, charities or private endowments, and increasingly corporate sponsorship. This depends of course on such sources of funding being available, which is often not the case in less economically advanced countries.

The value of special short-term grants is a matter of timing. They can be a very good stimulus for getting institutions started in using e-learning, as the institutions do not have to give up anything to do it. Such grants can also be useful to supplement or enhance other activities already funded by the institution. There is less risk attached to this kind of funding. If the project does not produce the results hoped for, the institution is not committed to continuing the activity.

However, by its nature, such funding is short-term, and limited in duration. Short-term grants raise the question of sustainability. What happens when the funds run out? Successful projects then become a real problem. How does the institution continue or extend the project? Furthermore, such grants tend to reflect the needs and priorities of the sponsors. Especially with respect to corporate sponsorship, the funding may be just a smart means of marketing equipment or services.

Even more importantly, staff who work on such projects tend to be employed on a temporary basis. When the project ends, they leave, and thus the learning experience and knowledge gained from the project is often lost to the institution. Because e-learning presents new challenges, there are proportionately few professionals with good experience and knowledge in this field. It is therefore all the more important that there is continuity and a chance to gain knowledge and experience, and to retain that, within an organization committed to the use of e-learning. Short-term funding makes this difficult, if not impossible.

Lastly, externally funded projects can float along on the sidelines, without affecting the 'core' activities of the institution. They can be safely ignored, whether or not they are successful.

Thus while the use of special external funding can be very useful, it should not be the only strategy for funding.

Increased government baseline funding for institutions

If the aim of supporting e-learning is to improve the quality of learning and to prepare students better for a knowledge-based society, rather than to save money, then it could be argued that **governments**

have a responsibility to face up to the additional costs that are necessary to support e-learning.

It has been argued (Bates, 2000) that institutions need to increase their teaching budgets by around 5 per cent to provide the necessary technical and production resources needed to support adequately an institution-wide initiative in e-learning.

Thus government may agree to increase baseline budgets by a small margin (1-2 per cent) for those institutions that can show a clear plan for the development of e-learning, and the associated additional costs that this would require. Increased government base funding for an institution could be dependent on the following:

- the institution has a clear plan and rationale for e-learning;
- the institution can clearly identify the extra costs and benefits of e-learning;
- the institution has made some difficult reallocation decisions or has found some additional resources of its own to support e-learning;
- there is evidence of student, parent and employer support for e-learning.

These funds would be needed in addition to the funds required to maintain the technological infrastructure, which could add another 5-10 per cent to annual operating costs. Thus governments should ask institutions not just for a five-year technology plan, but also for a five-year plan for teaching with technologies. Such plans would need to demonstrate the link between technological investment and potential learning outcomes, and the relative priorities for infrastructure and teaching support.

Government funding based on an institution's five-year IT and learning technologies plan would have the following advantage:

- it would encourage institutions to link technology investment to educational benefits;
- it would encourage the development of plans for e-learning;
- it would ensure that institutions have the technical capacity to support e-learning;

- it would ensure that some of the costs of e-learning are being accommodated by internal reallocation within the institution;
- it would ensure that institutional technology plans reflect the true cost of operation of e-learning.

Most importantly, it would put e-learning on a sustainable funding basis within those institutions committed to e-learning.

The drawback to such a strategy is that governments may not have the additional money or be able to make the necessary reallocations without damaging other high-priority programmes. Giving institutions even small increases in funding may discourage institutions from becoming more cost efficient. Such a strategy may also underestimate the savings possible on the indirect costs of face-to-face teaching available through a more aggressive move to e-learning.

However, given current knowledge about costs, this is a realistic, pragmatic strategy to kick-start institutions into e-learning. Institutional funding in any case is likely to be adjusted in subsequent years for a host of other reasons.

Use e-learning to absorb extra enrolments

Many governments, particularly in the less economically advanced countries, are facing a huge demand for post-secondary education. Even in some economically advanced jurisdictions, such as California and Florida in the USA, demand for access to universities and colleges will explode over the next 10 years, due to population growth. At the same time, in many economically advanced countries, a very high proportion of faculty and senior administrators is due to retire within the next five years. Thus many jurisdictions are facing major capacity problems.

It has already been indicated that there are high overhead and indirect costs in campus-based higher education, and that it is possible (though yet to be confirmed) that the overhead costs for e-learning will be lower. Thus one strategy would be to maintain or slightly increase the current level of face-to-face teaching, but absorb the additional numbers by a move to e-learning.

As an example, the University of Central Florida in Orlando has moved heavily to on-line learning to enable it to increase capacity from 35,000 to 60,000 students over five years; it simply cannot build enough fast enough to meet this expansion through face-to-face, campus-based teaching. Also, much of the demand is coming from those already in the workforce, in the high-tech sector, wishing to upgrade or pay their way through university.

Hoping that e-learning will bring down the average cost per student, and thus will be able to absorb all the extra demand at a lower cost, is a high-risk strategy for the long-term development of a post-secondary education system. Although desperate situations call for desperate measures, it is important that such a decision is based on careful research and national planning. Probably a mix of extra physical places and e-learning would be a safer strategy. It would be a foolish strategy if the dependency on e-learning to absorb extra numbers is not balanced by increased access to the technology within the general public.

Encourage cost-recoverable e-learning programmes

In most countries, the traditional market for post-secondary education is the student going straight from high school to university or college. In more economically advanced countries, there has been a tendency in recent years to fund a higher proportion of the costs through tuition fees. However, covering the full cost of a university or college education is beyond the means of most families if the student has no other source of income than family support or even part-time work. Given that there are not likely to be major savings through the use of e-learning, **expecting all e-learning programmes to cover their cost through student tuition fees is unrealistic.**

Nevertheless, for the lifelong learning market focused on people who may have already been subsidized through university or college, and are now working full time, it would not be unreasonable to expect them to cover the full cost of continuing education. This is not an issue specifically for e-learning, but the difference is that e-learning offers many benefits for those working and with families, compared with regular attendance at a campus. Thus for such a market, public-sector institutions could cover the full costs of e-learning from student tuition fees, if they are allowed to charge what the market will bear.

There are nevertheless often many barriers to prevent public institutions from running fully cost-recoverable or profit-generating programmes. First of all, government regulations often prevent institutions from offering non-credit programming, or require all new degree programmes to go through a lengthy, bureaucratic procedure for approval. Governments often regulate the fee levels for all degree programmes, irrespective of the target group. Sometimes government regulations explicitly prevent publicly funded institutions from running cost-recoverable or profit-generating programmes, or require any revenues for such programmes to be returned to government.

Thus governments could conduct a review of their regulations regarding programming aimed at the lifelong learning market, to make it easier for public-sector institutions to enter this market. This would be a way to encourage institutions to develop e-learning programmes without any additional net cost to government or the institution.

Another major barrier to operating cost-recoverable programmes is finding the start-up funding. Even in institutions with dedicated e-learning units and a technology infrastructure already in place, sums of $100,000 upwards may be required to develop programmes before any revenues can be generated.

There are several ways of finding start-up money, all of which mean investing unused or 'soft' money. Funds may have been allocated for projects, or set aside for major investments, and will be used in the future, but these funds sit in an account unused for short periods of time. A large university is likely to have significant amounts of money allocated to projects but unspent, or carried forward from one year to another (colleges tend to have less flexibility). Often this money is invested in short-term bonds then cashed when needed.

These 'soft' funds could be allocated to the start-up of a cost-recoverable project. The funds are used to cover all the costs of the programme, including the hiring of new research faculty if necessary. The borrowed funds are then paid back, with interest at market or below market rates, when the students pay their fees. Once the borrowed funds are repaid, the student fees cover the ongoing costs of the programme. There is a revenue sharing agreement that ensures that a substantial proportion of any profits goes back to the departments that create the programmes, thus providing incentives. This is how the University of British Columbia funds its cost-recoverable distance education e-learning programmes.

There is obviously some risk in this form of activity. Such projects need a well-prepared and researched business plan, and borrowing must not exceed the level where the institution as a whole cannot cover the risk. This strategy only works for those programmes where students can cover the full costs of programming, including institutional overheads and interest payments. Competition keeps margins tight. It needs very good management of projects, and administrative systems that track costs and revenues accurately. This strategy can be used for only a narrow range of programming aimed at 'niche' markets that can afford to pay.

Nevertheless this strategy allows new programmes to be developed without the need to take faculty away from their other activities such as research and face-to-face teaching, and enables e-learning to be started up and maintained without net cost to an institution.

Allow public institutions to establish for-profit companies

Start-up and initial operating funds may be obtained by borrowing money from outside the institution at market rates. This may be from banks or other financial institutions or through partnership with a venture capital company. In order to do this, a government-regulated public-sector institution will probably have to set up a separate for-profit company, to limit the risk to the institution, and to avoid breaking government financial regulations. This is one way to draw in new funds, and the pressure of a commercial for-profit operation may lead to a better understanding of how to operate more efficiently the non-profit e-learning activities in the conventional institution.

However, there are even more risks for an institution than in the previous strategy. It means handing over substantial sums to set up such a company, which may never be returned (there are already several examples of universities who have done this in the USA and lost all their investment). Such a company is more likely to be driven by the need for profit than meeting educational needs, whereas the previous strategy of cost-recovery has been used to support desired programming for which funds from other sources are unavailable.

More importantly, with a for-profit company, the rest of the institution remains untouched by innovation or e-learning or, worse, academic departments find themselves competing for the same clients as the for-profit company. Academic departments may indeed find themselves being undercut by the for-profit company, or have problems in meeting their own teaching commitments, if the for-profit company hires lower cost part-time or contract subject experts, or gets faculty to 'moonlight' for it.

Key issues and conclusions

In most countries, public-sector college and university degree programmes are heavily subsidized by government grants, in order to keep down the cost of tuition to students. The grant funding in many jurisdictions is based on an average cost per full-time student equivalent (FTE).

This has several consequences for e-learning. The jury is still out on whether e-learning is more or less expensive than face-to-face teaching. The evidence to date does not suggest that e-learning is a cheap alternative to the direct costs of face-to-face teaching, although the methods for costing both face-to-face teaching and e-learning are by no means clear or agreed. However, there is enough evidence (see for instance, Bartolic and Bates, 1999, and Whalen and Wright, 2000) to suggest that the costs for e-learning are different from those for face-to-face teaching.

This makes the application of funding formulae for face-to-face teaching difficult to apply to e-learning, especially when e-learning is focused on fully distance students. In particular, the ratio between direct and indirect costs seems to vary considerably between the two forms of teaching. More research and better costing methodologies that take into account direct and indirect costs are needed.

However, as institutions gradually combine face-to-face teaching with e-learning, the separation of funding policy between the two will become more difficult. Nevertheless, because of the known costs of start-up, and because of the need to develop sustainable forms of e-learning, funding strategies specifically to support e-learning need to be developed. Without specific actions to provide funding for e-learning, it is likely to remain a cottage industry, dependent on the goodwill and extra work of faculty and instructors.

There are also clearly major opportunities for the development of fully cost-recoverable e-learning programmes. This allows for new markets to be opened and, in particular, the lifelong learning market. Governments may need to look at how they regulate investment and borrowing in public institutions, to encourage a more entrepreneurial approach to on-line learning. Nevertheless, **the risks in entrepreneurial approaches to e-learning should not be underestimated.** The market is increasingly competitive. Many areas of public higher education are unlikely to be able to cover their costs, either through e-learning or face-to-face teaching, especially when student tuition fees are regulated.

In those areas such as lifelong learning and continuing professional education, where there are opportunities for at least cost-recovery, competition from both the public-sector and private-sector organizations is likely to be strong and hence margins low. **The ability to recover costs and make profits will depend, as in all markets, on price, quality of service, and value to the client.** This is likely to depend just as much on effective and high quality e-learning design, good on-line administrative systems, and strong management and financial strategies, as on outstanding academic content. Appropriate funding strategies then are likely to be critical for success.

Funding decisions are the most important strategy open to governments wishing to move institutions into (or away from) e-learning. **A major test of commitment to the use of e-learning is the extent to which governments and institutions are willing to use regular operating budgets to support such activities.**

It is also worth noting that the kind of people needed to support e-learning are highly skilled and in short supply, and that there is a steep learning curve in using new technologies for teaching. Therefore, **funding strategies should enable institutions to attract and retain good staff in these areas.** This is best done through regular or permanent positions rather than short-term funding, and **that requires allocation of funds to e-learning on a regular and recurring basis.**

Given the uncertainties around the costs and benefits of e-learning, government needs to be very clear as to the reasons for supporting or deciding not to support e-learning. This will be discussed in the final chapter.

VII. Policy issues for national leaders

The policy issue with respect to e-learning for all countries, rich or poor, is not one of direction but of readiness and scale. At what point should a nation start investing in e-learning? The short answer is immediately, but not for everyone in the country.

Are you ready for e-learning?

The first question that needs to be asked is whether a country is ready to create or exploit a knowledge-based economy. One of the major reasons for introducing e-learning is to better prepare for a knowledge-based economy. E-learning is like helping children learn to swim, by letting them play in the water. It is the right environment for learning how to operate in a knowledge-based society, not just for work but also for life. **Those countries that are not yet ready for the knowledge-based economy are probably not yet ready for e-learning.**

Most developing countries do not have the resources, the technology infrastructure or the skilled workforce necessary to make e-learning available on a wide scale, at least for many years. When resources are scarce, they need to be concentrated and very carefully focused.

This makes it all the more important that governments base e-learning policy decisions on careful research into the different markets for post-secondary education and training, and what the private sector will pay for. Governments need to base their decisions on e-learning strategy on students' likely access to technology in the future, the overall costs, including overheads, of both face-to-face teaching and e-learning, the benefits and disadvantages of different methods of delivery, and their appropriateness for the national economy. One way of reducing the risk would be by focusing e-learning on the lifelong learning market, since those in this market are more likely to have access to the technology, and are more able to pay the cost.

Traditional schools, open universities, or virtual education?

One major issue is the balance between investment in e-learning, compared with investment in either traditional campus-based education, or in the more traditional print- and broadcasting-based open universities.

Studies by Rumble (1997) and others have shown that the print- and broadcasting-based open universities offer considerable cost and sometimes quality advantages over conventional campus-based education, due to the economies of scale of the open universities.

These cost advantages over conventional education are not so apparent with high quality e-learning. The big difference between e-learning and open universities is the direct interaction between the instructor and the students in e-learning, leading to more individualized instruction. This encourages critical thinking skills, good communication skills, problem-solving skills, the ability to work in a team, and eventually the ability to take responsibility for learning and personal action, all the skills needed in a knowledge-based economy.

This however comes at a cost. Although there are some economies of scale compared with conventional education, e-learning requires a reasonable student/teacher ratio to avoid instructors becoming swamped with e-mail and discussion forum messages. What e-learning is offering is a more interactive education encouraging critical thinking, communication skills, and flexibility for both students and teachers, compared with the one-way mass media of open universities.

Thus **for countries with large numbers of students unable to access the later years of secondary or higher education, the open university model is likely to be the most appropriate**, particularly if the aim is to develop a mass skilled workforce able to work in traditional industries or services. Open universities such as the Alama Iqbal Open University in Pakistan, then, still provide the best route for mass education (see Daniel, 1998, for further development of this argument).

However, for countries that already have reasonable access to secondary and higher education, and a reasonable Internet infrastructure, e-learning will provide advantages over both conventional and open universities. These advantages will increase particularly for those countries wishing to move into a knowledge-based economy, but where there is a shortage of well-qualified teachers, since students can access e-learning from anywhere in the world. **Countries** such as India, China, South Africa, Malaysia, Thailand, Brazil, and Mexico, **with a burgeoning e-commerce business sector, a growing indigenous high-tech sector, a fast-developing middle class, and a rapidly developing Internet infrastructure, will need to move more and more into e-learning.**

Infrastructure or education?

E-learning is heavily dependent on appropriate technological infrastructure already being in place for commercial or government reasons. **Stable electricity supply and reliable and moderately priced Internet access is a necessary condition for e-learning.**

It has been shown earlier that government can certainly develop policies that will encourage a rapid growth of the Internet. Some governments have made the decision to invest heavily themselves in the basic infrastructure, because of lack of investment by the private sector. The trick here is to know when to open up the management of Internet services to the private sector, once a market has been created. Government's main responsibility though is to do what it can to widen access to the technology, through opening up the telecommunications market to competition, and through regulation of services.

However, until there is a basic and reliable Internet infrastructure in place, connecting at a minimum to most key businesses and universities, e-learning is unlikely to be a realistic or practical choice for most learners.

The need for a skilled workforce to support e-learning

Even if the infrastructure is in place, there must be a capacity to supply the necessary trained people to support and sustain e-learning.

As well as technically trained people who can install, manage and maintain the necessary technical infrastructure, e-learning also needs skilled media producers, such as Web designers and instructional designers. Professors and instructors need to be convinced of the value of e-learning, and trained to understand its educational and technical requirements. Managers need to understand the costs and benefits and the necessary means of working to exploit e-learning fully. Above all, senior institutional management requires vision and leadership, to see how e-learning can transform its institutions and provide graduates with a competitive edge.

Unfortunately, there is a global shortage of people with these skills. The danger is that a country will provide the necessary training, then those trained will emigrate to countries able to pay more for their services. Nevertheless, **without** such **a skilled workforce to support it, e-learning will not work.**

Developing a minimal e-learning strategy

Even the poorest countries probably cannot afford to ignore totally the potential of e-learning. At least its leaders need to be computer literate, to know how to use and navigate the Internet, and to understand not just the technology, but its importance for national development. The minimum then that most countries should do is to ensure that key government offices, businesses and universities have Internet access.

Even in the least developed countries economically, there are likely to be small sectors or pockets where telecommunications companies, on-line services, international corporations, government computer services, small businesses, and so forth require skilled people who can work in a knowledge-based environment. There may be small businesses that can grow into larger business on a national basis that would benefit from highly skilled people taught through e-learning. In particular, young people are highly motivated to play and work with computers. E-learning could provide tremendous opportunities for bringing otherwise unmotivated, unemployed youth into a working, highly productive economy, even – or especially – in the poorest countries.

If e-learning represents a significant element of the future of education, as seems increasingly likely, **the sooner that a nation or an education system gains experience and practice in e-learning, the more economically competitive that nation is likely to become.** The reverse is also true: ignoring the impact of e-learning on post-secondary education and training could substantially reduce a nation's ability to compete economically in the twenty-first century. The gap between rich and poor will continue to widen.

The role of the university in particular is important. A prestigious conventional national university mandated to provide national leadership in e-learning, or a specially created national e-university, can provide a model of the benefits and services available through the Internet. Such institutions can develop at least an elite with the skills needed to service national technical and educational needs for information technology development and for e-learning.

This will enable the nation to build an affordable and targeted technology infrastructure, to participate in regional collaborative projects, to develop partnerships with institutions in other countries, to identify and adapt suitable programmes from other countries, and to develop its own programmes where appropriate.

Global debates around e-learning

E-learning also raises some uncomfortable policy issues that the international community has yet to resolve successfully. Some of these are general issues of globalization. E-learning however is both an example of how these issues play out in reality, as well as forcing debate on these very issues.

In particular, what can countries do to protect their national post-secondary institutions, culture and language when faced with the threat of foreign educational programmes through e-learning – especially if national students perceive economic and financial advantages from taking out-of-state qualifications through e-learning?

To what extent should e-learning be privatized and what will the impact be on publicly funded institutions? For countries with few resources, it will be tempting to allow the international private sector in to provide international-standard e-learning to those who can afford to pay for it.

To what extent will for-profit e-learning activities by public institutions lead to pressure to open up educational services as a trade, governed by the World Trade Organization and the General Agreement on Tariffs and Trades? For instance, will private multinational corporations be able to complain about unfair competition from state-subsidized institutions?

What is the tax status of public universities that set up for-profit operations? Should government take into account revenues generated by for-profit activities when deciding on state budget allocations to an institution?

To what extent should private-sector investment and partnership be encouraged? What safeguards (if any) are required when partnering with a commercial organization? Does commercial partnership inevitably corrupt or distort the fundamental values of a university or college? If so, in what ways?

Different governments will answer these questions differently, according to different political ideologies and positions. All these and probably many more questions need broader debate. UNESCO could play an important role in providing a forum for such discussion between nations.

Conclusion

It is clear that information technology capacity will continue to expand at a rapid rate throughout the world. This will be driven primarily for commercial purposes, but it will also provide the opportunity for economically important e-learning developments. Probably **no country can afford to ignore the impact of the Internet on post-secondary education and training.**

However, e-learning requires a very stringent set of conditions for it to work successfully. For these conditions to be met, there is a high cost in terms of investment and training. Most important of all, the technological infrastructure must be in place. While the technology underpinning e-learning is developing and spreading rapidly, the most valuable developments are not yet commercially available or developed for those that most need it: the poor and those excluded from post-secondary education.

E-learning is not the answer to many of the most pressing educational problems faced particularly by poorer developing nations. Other strategies, such as open universities, can provide greater access and more cost-effective delivery of education.

Governments however can do much to encourage the right environment for e-learning. Indeed, governments cannot afford not to expose at least a minimum number of its nationals to the benefits of e-learning. **The poorer the country, the more focused its efforts to support e-learning will need to be.** Partnership with institutions and governments in more developed countries, collaboration between countries with similar cultures and stages of economic development, and well-targeted, small-scale projects will all help develop capacity and skills in e-learning.

In particular, small states within regions need to collaborate and share resources. Regional e-universities carefully focused on specific target groups, backed by government assistance in providing suitable technology access, could be one way forward. The international community could also do more to help by directly assisting countries to develop Internet and e-learning capacity, and providing the necessary resources to widen access to the poorest sectors of society. **We have a responsibility to ensure that all benefit in the twenty-first century.**

References

American Productivity & Quality Centre. 1999. *Today's teaching and learning: leveraging technology: best practice report*. Houston: The American Productivity & Quality Centre.

Arnove, R. 1976. *Educational television: a policy critique and guide for developing countries*. New York: Praeger.

Bartolic, S.; Bates, A. 1999. "Investing in online learning: potential benefits and limitations". In: *Canadian Journal of Communication, 24*, pp. 349-366.

Bates, A. 2000. *Managing technological change: strategies for college and university leaders*. San Francisco: Jossey Bass.

Conference Board of Canada. 1991. *Employability skill profile: the critical skills required of the Canadian workforce*. Ottawa: Conference Board of Canada.

Daniel, J. 1998. *Mega-universities and knowledge media: technology strategies for higher education*. London: Kogan Page.

Dirr, P. 2001. "The development of new organizational arrangements in virtual learning". In: Farrell, G. (Ed.), *The changing faces of virtual education*. Vancouver, B.C.: Commonwealth of Learning.

Dziuban, C.; Hartman, J.; Juge, F.; Moskal, P.; Sorg, S.; Truman-Davis, B. 1999. "Faculty development, learner support and evaluation in Web-based programs". In: *Interactive Learning Environments (The Netherlands), 7*(2&3), pp. 137-154.

Government of British Columbia. 2000. *Educational technology policy framework*. Victoria, B.C.: Government of British Columbia, Ministry of Advanced Education (http://www.aved.gov.bc.ca/strategic/edtech/execsum/execsum.pdf).

Harasim, L.; Hiltz, S.; Teles, L.; Turoff, M. 1995. *Learning networks.* Cambridge, MA: The MIT Press.

Hope, A. 2001. "Quality Assurance". In: Farrell, G. (Ed.), *The changing face of virtual education.* Vancouver, B.C.: Commonwealth of Learning.

Institute for Higher Education Policy. 2001. *Quality on the line.* Institute for Higher Education Policy (http://www.ihep.com/Pubs/PDF/Quality.pdf).

Karelis, C. 1999. "Education technology and cost control: four models". In: *Syllabus, 12*(6), February 1999.

Moe, M.; Blodget, H. 2000. *The knowledge Web.* New York: Merrill Lynch.

Mugridge, I.; Kaufman, D. (Eds.). 1986. *Distance education in Canada.* London: Croom Helm.

Naidoo, V. 2000. "The changing venues for learning". In: Farrell, G. (Ed.), *The changing faces of virtual education.* Vancouver, B.C.: Commonwealth of Learning.

Oblinger, D.; Barone, C.; Hawkins, B. 2001. *Distributed education and its challenges.* Washington, D.C.: American Council for Education.

Perry, W.G. Jr. 1970. *Forms of intellectual and ethical development in the college years: a scheme.* New York: Holt, Rinehart and Winston.

Porter, D. 2001. "Object lessons from the Web". In: Farrell, G. (Ed.), *The changing faces of virtual education.* Vancouver, B.C.: Commonwealth of Learning.

Quality Assurance Agency for Higher Education. 1999. *Guidelines on the quality assurance of distance education.* Gloucester, UK: Quality Assurance Agency for Higher Education (http://www.qaa.ac.uk/public/dlg/append1.htm).

Rogers, E. 1995. *The diffusion of innovations*. New York: Free Press.

Rumble, G.; Harry, K. 1982. *The distance teaching universities*. London: Croom Helm.

Russell, T. 1999. *The no significant difference phenomenon*. Raleigh, NC: Office of Instructional Communications, North Carolina State University.

Sharma, R. 2001. "Online delivery of programmes: a case study of Indira Gandhi National Open University" In: *International Review of Research in Open and Distance Learning, 1*(2).

Whalen, T.; Wright, D. 2000. *The business case for Web-based training*. Norwood, MA: Artech House.

Appendix: Summary of research into the costs of e-learning

There have been several extensive studies on the costs of distance education and the use of mass communications technologies for post-secondary education and training. Rumble (1997) has written the most extensive study on the costs of open and distance learning, but it does not directly address the costs of e-learning, focusing mainly on print and broadcast delivery. Rumble built on earlier studies of the cost-effectiveness of the British Open University (Wagner, 1972, 1982; Laidlaw and Layard, 1974).

The World Bank commissioned UNESCO to undertake a number of studies in the early 1980s on the cost-effectiveness of mass communications technologies such as television and radio in education in developing countries (UNESCO, 1980, 1982). These studies built on the earlier work of Jamison, Klees and Wells from Stanford University (Jamison, 1977; Jamison and Klees, 1973; Klees and Wells, 1977, 1980). Orivel (1987) summarized and critiqued this research.

Potashnik and Adkins (1996) of the World Bank followed up on these studies by looking at the costs of applying information technologies to teaching and learning in developing countries, but this study largely preceded the development of e-learning over the Web.

Bates (1995) provided a detailed cost and benefit comparison between print, radio, audio-cassettes, audio-conferencing, broadcast TV, video-conferencing, video-cassettes, CD-ROMs, and computer-mediated communication, but did not cover Web-based programming.

Hülsmann (2000) provides a useful comparison of costs for different technologies, based on the costs derived from 11 case studies using different technologies for delivering open learning. However only one of his case studies, a joint graduate programme from the University of Maryland (USA) and the University of Oldenburg (Germany), was based on using the Web for delivery.

Bartolic and Bates (1999) published a paper based on the analysis of costs from two Web-based university graduate courses in Canada (the University of British Columbia and the University of Toronto), which can be found at http://det.cstudies.ubc.ca/detsite/framewhat-index.html.

Whalen and Wright (2000) have set out the business case for Web-based training, based on the case of the Bell Canada Online Institute. Finkelstein et al. (2000) provide 15 essays on detailed case studies, cost equations, planning and accounting methodologies with respect to the use of e-learning in colleges and universities in the United States of America.

An article in the Chronicle of Higher Education (16 February, 2001) reported on six studies commissioned by the Alfred P. Sloan Foundation that explored the financial costs and potential profitability of distance learning at six universities. Most of the reports – based on studies conducted at the Rochester Institute of Technology, the University of Illinois at Urbana-Champaign, the University of Maryland's University College, and Drexel, Pace, and Pennsylvania State Universities – reveal that the universities are hovering close to the break-even point with their distance-learning programmes. How well the programmes appear to be doing depends, in part, on how their costs and revenues are defined. The Andrew Mellon Foundation has also funded research on the cost-effectiveness of technology in higher education, but has not to date published any hard data.

Frank Jewett conducted 12 case studies of technology-based teaching in universities and colleges in the USA. From these studies Jewett developed a simulation model (BRIDGE) for comparing the cost of expanding a campus using distributed instruction versus classroom instruction (Jewett, 1999).

It would be fair to say that most of the research on the costs or the cost-effectiveness of e-learning is either work in progress, or based on relatively small samples or cases, often unpublished or not published in refereed journals. Most of the published studies are on the use of the Web for 'pure' distance education. There is almost no substantive research study yet on the costs of Web-based 'mixed-mode' teaching.

Summarizing the costs and benefits of on-line learning

A typical on-line distance education course at UBC would have the following components:

- three credits (1/40 of an undergraduate, four-year bachelor's degree);
- one semester in length (13 weeks);
- a project management approach (research professor, instructional designer, Web programmer);
- relatively modest multimedia requirements (e.g. text, some graphics, a few carefully selected audio and video clips, some minor Java-based student interaction with the Web site, e.g. tests, exercises);
- WebCT as the basic platform but modified to meet the specific needs of the course;
- course enrolment of 40 students per offering, once per year, over five years;
- two tutors: the research professor who designed the course plus a part-time instructor with a Ph.D.; hence a 1:20 teacher/student ratio;
- each tutor would supervise an on-line discussion forum of 20 students;
- three written assignments, one of which would be a three-student group assignment.

The total direct costs of such a course (including the time of all the university staff) over five years would be about $120,000, or $24,000 a year. Development (including course maintenance), hence fixed costs, would constitute about 50 per cent of this cost ($60,000), and delivery (variable costs) about 50 per cent ($60,000). The average cost per student for 40 students per course offering over five years would be approximately $600 ($120,000/200). If 60 students a year were enrolled, with an additional part-time instructor hired, the development costs would remain unchanged (at approximately $60,000) but the delivery costs would increase from $60,000 to $90,000 over five years. Thus the average cost per student would be $500 ($150,000/300). It can be seen then that the cost per student would drop, thus achieving some economies of scale, as numbers increase.

There are problems though in trying to compare this with the cost of teaching an equivalent face-to-face class at UBC. This is because the above costs do not include university overheads, which make up 47 per cent of the costs of face-to-face instruction at UBC. Also costs vary a great deal from department to department. It would be important to match carefully the on-line course with an equivalent face-to-face course. Unfortunately the comparable data for face-to-face teaching did not exist in the form necessary for a fair comparison when the on-line cost data were collected.

The comparison with the former print-based courses also has to be somewhat qualitative. The fixed costs of developing Web-based courses were somewhat lower, and the maintenance costs higher, than print. The delivery costs however were higher for the Web courses, because of the need for a lower teacher/student ratio for the on-line discussion forums and interaction with the instructors.

Bartolic and Bates (1999) not only reported on the above costs for a graduate-level non-credit course aimed at working professionals, but also measured benefits. The main benefits of the on-line courses were:

- increased access for part-time students, and for full-time students with timetabling or part-time work conflicts;
- access to out-of-province and international students;
- improved written communication skills;
- much increased participation by students in discussion through the on-line discussion forums, compared with print-based distance education;
- greater interaction with the instructors than print-based distance education;
- by widening the market beyond the province, the course comfortably covered its direct costs from student fees, although it is not clear whether all overhead costs would have been recovered as well.

Implications for national strategies for e-learning

The research and experience to date suggest that the costs of face-to-face teaching, traditional mass media/print-based distance learning, and distance e-learning can be summarized by the following conceptual diagram (*Figure 3*):

Figure 3.   Comparative costs of different modes of delivery

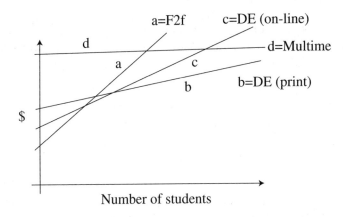

If we look at the average cost per student, we can see that for face-to-face teaching (a), fixed costs (buildings, equipment, etc.) are relatively low, but *if teacher/student ratios are maintained* costs increase proportionate to the increase in the number of students. (It is more of a step function – for every 20, 30 or 40 students, another teacher is hired).

If we look at the traditional print-based, mass-media model of distance education, as practised by many of the national open universities (b), we can see that fixed costs are much higher than for face-to-face teaching, but marginal costs for additional students are much lower.

For on-line distance education (c), the fixed costs are higher than for face-to-face teaching, but lower than for mass-media, print-based distance education. However, because of the need to keep teacher/student ratios relatively low for on-line learning, the variable costs are higher than for print-based distance education, but lower than for face-to-face teaching, as numbers increase.

Lastly, if we look at the cost of multimedia (d), such as CD-ROMs, combining lots of video perhaps with large quantities of graphics or data, or complex interactions such as expert systems or simulations, then the fixed cost is very high. However, the delivery cost of a CD-ROM or Internet delivery is very low. Note though that if an instructor was to be provided, the multimedia costs would need to be combined with those for on-line learning.

Although *Figure 3* is conceptual, and the actual lines and particularly the cut-off points will vary from system to system, the relationship between the cost structures are well supported by the research. However, Karelis (1999) makes an excellent point when he states:

> "the crossover point of the two delivery systems [face-to-face compared with technology delivery] generally falls to the right of what I am going to call the 'scale barrier', or the current practical upper limit on the number of student enrolments. In other words, it is only at an enrolment level that is rarely reached that the cost of the classroom delivery system exceeds that of the capital-intensive delivery system. So, in most cases capital-intensive technology cannot lower the average cost per-student below the cost of classroom instruction. Whatever other benefit it affords, technology does not offer any economic cost advantage. To summarize, instruction seldom hits the enrolment level needed to make capital-intensive technology-mediated instruction economical."

The large distance education universities have been able to avoid Karelis' criticism because they have put in place completely different structures from conventional universities, and thus have managed to enrol very large numbers of students. However, most on-line learning has been focused in dual-mode or conventional higher education institutions. Without a major restructuring, they will not achieve the student numbers necessary to reduce average costs. A central distance education unit, as at UBC, is one way to do this. Undergraduate enrolments through the Distance Education and Technology unit at UBC have increased by 49 per cent over the four years from 1997 to 2001, giving the necessary economies of scale in most of its courses to make its courses cheaper per student than the equivalent face-to-face courses. With its cost-recoverable courses, DE&T has deliberately gone out-of-province and international to ensure that its numbers are viable. In most cases, however, where on-line learning is part of a department's normal teaching load, and focused on its already enrolled students, it is unlikely to generate the extra enrolments to be cost-effective.

Appendix references

Bartolic, S.; Bates, A. 1999. "Investing in online learning: potential benefits and limitations". *Canadian Journal of Communication, 24*, pp. 349-366.

Bates, A. 1995. *Technology, open learning and distance education.* London: Routledge.

Finkelstein, M.; Frances, C.; Jewett, F.; Scholz, M. 2000. *Dollars, distance, and online education: the new economics of college teaching and learning.* Westport, Conn.: American Council on Education/Oryx Press.

Hülsmann, T. 2000. *The costs of open learning: a handbook.* Oldenburg: Bibliotheks- und Informationssystem der Universität Oldenburg.

Jamison, D. 1977. *Cost factors in planning educational technology systems.* Paris: UNESCO.

Jamison, D.; Klees, S. 1973. *The cost of instructional radio and television for developing countries.* Stanford: Stanford University, Institute for Communications Research.

Jewett, F. 1999. *BRIDGE: A campus cost simulation model for comparing the costs of mediated instruction with traditional lecture/lab methods.* Seal Beach, CA: CSU/CO.

Karelis, C. 1999. "Education technology and cost control: four models". In: *Syllabus, 12*(6), February, 1999.

Klees, S.; Wells, S. 1977. *Cost effectiveness and cost benefit analysis for educational planning and evaluation: methodology and application to instructional technology.* Washington, D.C.: USAID.

Klees, S.; Wells, S. 1980. *Economic analysis and education: critical issues in application to instructional technology.* Paris: UNESCO.

Laidlaw, B.; Layard, R. 1974. "Traditional versus Open University teaching method: a cost comparison". In: *Review of Educational Research, 61*(2), pp. 179-211.

Orivel, F. 1987. *Costs and effectiveness of distance teaching systems.* Dijon: IREDU.

Potashnik, M.; Adkins, D. 1996. "Cost analysis of information technology projects in education: experiences from developing countries". In: *Education and Technology Series, 1*(1). Washington, D.C.: World Bank.

Rumble, G. 1997. *The costs and economics of open and distance learning.* London: Kogan Page.

UNESCO. 1980. *The economics of educational media. Vol. 2: Cost and effectiveness.* Paris: UNESCO.

UNESCO. 1982. *The economics of educational media. Vol. 3: Cost and effectiveness overview and synthesis.* Paris: UNESCO.

Wagner, L. 1972. "The economics of the Open University". In: *Higher Education, 1*, pp. 159-183.

Wagner, L. 1982. *The economics of educational media.* London: Macmillan.

Whalen, T.; Wright, D. 2000. *The business case for Web-based training.* Norwood, MA: Artech House.

IIEP publications and documents

More than 1,200 titles on all aspects of educational planning have been published by the International Institute for Educational Planning. A comprehensive catalogue is available in the following subject categories:

Educational planning and global issues
General studies – global/developmental issues

Administration and management of education
Decentralization – participation – distance education – school mapping – teachers

Economics of education
Costs and financing – employment – international co-operation

Quality of education
Evaluation – innovation – supervision

Different levels of formal education
Primary to higher education

Alternative strategies for education
Lifelong education – non-formal education – disadvantaged groups – gender education

Copies of the Catalogue may be obtained on request from:
IIEP, Dissemination of Publications
information@iiep.unesco.org
Titles of new publications and abstracts may be consulted at the
following Web site: *http://www.unesco.org/iiep*

The International Institute for Educational Planning

The International Institute for Educational Planning (IIEP) is an international centre for advanced training and research in the field of educational planning. It was established by UNESCO in 1963 and is financed by UNESCO and by voluntary contributions from Member States. In recent years the following Member States have provided voluntary contributions to the Institute: Denmark, Finland, Germany, Iceland, India, Ireland, Norway, Sweden and Switzerland.

The Institute's aim is to contribute to the development of education throughout the world, by expanding both knowledge and the supply of competent professionals in the field of educational planning. In this endeavour the Institute co-operates with interested training and research organizations in Member States. The Governing Board of the IIEP, which approves the Institute's programme and budget, consists of a maximum of eight elected members and four members designated by the United Nations Organization and certain of its specialized agencies and institutes.

Inquiries about the Institute should be addressed to:
The Office of the Director, International Institute for Educational Planning,
7-9 rue Eugène-Delacroix, 75116 Paris, France.

Imprimerie Alençonnaise
2, rue Édouard-Belin, 61002 Alençon
Dépôt légal : 2ᵉ trimestre 2002 - N° d'ordre : 50289